MAINSTREAMING THE LEARNING DISABLED ADOLESCENT

This manual was developed as a part of
South Carolina's Child Service Demonstration Center,
funded under Title VI-G from the
Bureau of Education for the Handicapped.

MAINSTREAMING THE LEARNING DISABLED ADOLESCENT

A Staff Development Guide

By

WILLIAM E. CHAIKEN, Ph.D.

South Carolina Region V Educational Services Center
Lancaster, South Carolina

and

MARY JOYCE HARPER, M.Ed.

South Carolina Region V Educational Services Center
Lancaster, South Carolina

CHARLES C THOMAS • PUBLISHER
Springfield • Illinois • U.S.A.

Published and Distributed Throughout the World by
CHARLES C THOMAS ● PUBLISHER
Bannerstone House
301-327 East Lawrence Avenue, Springfield, Illinois, U.S.A.

© *1979, by* CHARLES C THOMAS ● PUBLISHER

ISBN 0-398-03871-6

Library of Congress Catalog Card Number: 78-24289

With THOMAS BOOKS *careful attention is given to all details of
manufacturing and design. It is the Publisher's desire to present books that
are satisfactory as to their physical qualities and artistic possibilities and
appropriate for their particular use.* THOMAS BOOKS *will be true to those
laws of quality that assure a good name and good will.*

Printed in the United States of America
V-R-1

Library of Congress Cataloging in Publication Data
Chaiken, William E
    Mainstreaming the learning disabled adolescent.

    Bibliography: p. 143
    Includes index.
    1. Learning disabilities. 2. Mainstreaming in
education. I. Harper, Mary Joyce, joint author.
II. Title.
LC4704.C46   373.1'1'46   78-24289
ISBN 0-398-03871-6

INTRODUCTION

TEN years ago, most learning disabled students were being served in self-contained classrooms in the primary and elementary grades. With the emergence of the resource room concept in the early 1970s, the majority of these children began receiving remedial instruction in resource rooms while spending the major portion of the school day in regular classes. A few years later, these students appeared in the middle and junior high schools and, somewhat surprisingly, were still deficient in some or many of the basic skills. As it became apparent that these students were still in need of special help in order to survive in the middle and junior high schools, it also became apparent that there were other adolescents in the schools whose learning disabilities had not yet been discovered.

The program described in this manual is designed to serve mildly handicapped learning disabled (LD) students who would benefit from the services of a resource room while being placed in the mainstream of the middle school curriculum. Total staff involvement is seen as the key to a successful program and is the major focus of this book.

Part I of the book describes the special characteristics and needs of the adolescent learning disabled student. Although like the younger LD student in many ways, the older LD student brings many years of failure and frustration, compounded with the turmoil of adolescence, into the classrooms of our schools.

Ways of organizing and developing a middle school resource room program are described in Part II. Part III describes techniques for staff development for the effective mainstreaming of these students. Modification of teaching techniques are necessary for the older LD students, and one method of training teachers to provide these modifications is presented here. Techniques for evaluation of student achievement and program effectiveness are presented in Part IV.

Finally, Part V includes a suggested procedure for planning the implementation of a mainstreaming program. It is our sincere hope that this book will assist those already involved, and those who wish to become involved, in developing quality programs for the adolescent learning disabled student.

ACKNOWLEDGMENTS

THIS book was developed as an outgrowth of two years of intensive work with middle school teachers, counselors, and administrators in five South Carolina school districts. We wish to thank our colleagues in these districts for their dedication to providing exemplary services to the learning disabled students in their schools and for skillfully implementing the activities and procedures suggested in this book.

We wish to give special thanks to Bruce Ambrose, Marjorie Cochran, Barbara Howard, Libby McLean, Marlene Metts, and Don Neal for their assistance in the development of many of the ideas and activities that follow.

We extend our gratitude to Alice Warfield for her preparation of the manuscript with its many revisions.

W.E.C.
M.J.H.

CONTENTS

MAINSTREAMING THE
LEARNING DISABLED ADOLESCENT

(

PART I

CHARACTERISTICS
AND NEEDS
OF
LEARNING DISABLED
ADOLESCENTS

DURING the past few years, there has been much controversy over, and many attempts to develop, a universally accepted definition of learning disabilities. Attempts have also been made to operationalize existing definitions. The definition established by the National Advisory Committee on Handicapped Children (NACHC) in 1968, however, appears to be the most widely accepted definition at this time. This definition states:

> Learning disabilities pupils means pupils with special learning disabilities who exhibit a disorder in one or more of the basic psychological processes involved in understanding or in using spoken or written language. These may be manifested in disorders of listening, thinking, talking, reading, writing, spelling, or arithmetic. They include conditions which have been referred to as perceptual handicaps, brain injury, minimal brain dysfunction, dyslexia, developmental aphasia, etc. They do not include problems which are due primarily to visual, hearing, or motor handicaps, to mental retardation, emotional disturbance or environmental disadvantage.

While this definition is the one most accepted and most often used, it is interpreted differently by different people. Wiederholt (1975) believes, for example, that there are three basic ways in which the term *basic psychological processes* is interpreted. These three interpretations are (1) the neurological approach, (2) the psychological approach, and (3) the "school skills" approach. The neurological approach implies brain damage or brain dysfunction. Professionals who espouse the psychological viewpoint, according to Wiederholt, determine the presence of a process deficit by measuring underlying psychological "constructs," i.e. visual memory, visual perception, and auditory reception.

Professionals involved in the school skills approach "avoid neurological and psychological terminology and instead focus upon the specific skills in language, reading, writing, spelling, arithmetic, and school related behavior" (Wiederholt, 1975, p. 19). The school skills approach seems most appropriate for teachers, for they are concerned about what the student can and cannot do and methods and materials for remediation.

The search for the ideal definition will probably continue for some time. Once, if ever, a suitable definition of learning disabilities is developed and accepted, a need for school personnel to be aware of the special characteristics and needs presented by the adolescent learning disabled student will still exist.

Although specific behavioral characteristics of the older learning disabled student are difficult to define, Donald D. Deshler believes that a partial profile of these students is beginning to emerge. In an article entitled "Psycho-Social Characteristics of Learning Disabled Adolescents" (1975), Deshler lists the following characteristics:

> First, the performance profile of the learning disabled adolescent reflects a pattern of both strengths and weaknesses. Since some areas of functioning are within normal limits the educational treatment and prognosis suggested for these youngsters is markedly different from that indicated for youngsters with a profile that is suppressed in all areas of functioning.

> Second, many skills basic to the academic process are still lacking or have been incorrectly acquired. Success in the academic curriculum will be limited until sufficient survival skills and techniques are mastered which allow the student to function independently in an academic setting.

> Third, by adolescence there is a high probability that learning disabled students will experience the indirect effects of a learning handicap as manifested by poor self-perception,

lowered self-concept, or reduced motivation. While a disability in a basic learning process may be the root problem, it must be considered in relation to other problems which it may precipitate.

Finally, maturation and/or compensation tend to refine and integrate many psychological, perceptual, or motor functions. Consequently, problems of incoordination, hyperactivity, distractibility, and poor attention may manifest themselves in more subtle or controlled ways in older students. Still to be resolved, however, is whether these functions are refined significantly through maturation and/or compensation, so as to become normal behaviors rather than remaining as deviant characteristics. [p. 230]

The learning problems and behavioral charcteristics presented by any group of learning disabled students are diverse, and it is difficult to list characteristics when there is so much variation within a population. The following behavioral characteristics of learning disabled students are most often cited:

Hyperactivity
Perseveration
Lack of coordination
Emotional instability
Impulsiveness
Perceptual difficulties
Motor difficulties
Language difficulties

These characteristics, although often somewhat evident at the middle school level, have changed in degree and observability. For instance, Evangeline Wilcox (1970, p. 5), says of hyperactivity, "The teenaged (neurologically handicapped) person does not engage in the frantic to-and-fro purposeless motor activity that is seen in the five and six year old. He has responded to a number of influences such as discipline, personal dignity, and increased rationality, so that his urge for constant movement now is more sophisticated and is restricted to tapping (finger, pencils or feet), grimacing and tics."

The following checklist may be more appropriately used to sight frequent problems presented by the older learning disabled student:

- Discrepancy between written and oral response
- Discrepancy in performance in academic areas
- Difficulty in following directions
- Trouble in completing assignments
- Reading level substantially below grade placement
- Difficulty in attending to tasks
- Disorganization
- Poor handwriting
- Problems in reasoning abstractly
- Poor social skills
- Poor arithmetic skills
- Poor spelling

A student with any one or several of these problems needs special attention in the middle or junior high school he or she enters. Here he or she encounters numerous changes from the security of the elementary classroom. He or she now has five, six, or seven teachers who teach 150 to 160 students a day. These departmentalized teachers are many times unaware of the special needs of the LD student. They may find it extremely difficult to individualize instruction when there are so many students to see.

Teachers often lecture, and the LD student may have difficulty processing the spoken word — or trouble taking meaningful notes. He or she may not be able to read assignments and now has to keep up with books, schedules, and lockers. Now, more so than before, failing grades appear on test papers, written assignments, and report cards.

Usually, by getting to know students well, teachers can identify a student whose achievement is markedly below what one would expect. They can identify those who "have the information and can't express it verbally or get it down on paper — those who are restless when the teacher lectures, but can watch a film attentively and afterwards contribute to meaningful discussion — those who cannot read the text and thereby gain information, but can do well on an oral test after class discussion — those who do well in math until word problems are the assignment — those who spend fifteen minutes longer on one math example — those that they 'feel' can learn, but do not."

Hagin (1971, p. 13) says of the adolescent LD student, "Although he works hard he may find others, not any brighter than he, receive better marks on compositions and recitations because of their easy verbalization or free-flowing pens. Underlying all these problems, the adolescent may feel the nagging fear that he might not, after all, be very bright."

Because of these feelings and a general lowered self-perception due to repeated failure, learning disabled adolescents need individual and small group counseling and understanding teachers to help them realize their strengths, accept their weaknesses, and work effectively toward social adjustment and academic growth.

Remediation in a resource room setting coupled with curriculum adjustments in the regular classroom assures more success experiences for the LD student. Success enhances the self-perceptions of these youngsters. Counseling enhances continued growth in self-perception and social adjustment as these young people confront adolescence as learning disabled students.

PART II

RESOURCE
ROOM
PROGRAM

IN recent years, the resource room model has gained popularity as a means of providing remedial instruction to exceptional students while giving them the added advantages of regular classroom participation. In the preface of *The Resource Room: Rationale and Implementation* (Hammill and Wiederholt, 1972), the authors state that self-contained classrooms do not provide the best educational setting for the majority of exceptional children. They recommend the use of a resource room with the primary goal being "to provide the kind of instructional support to both the child and his classroom teacher that makes feasible the pupil's continued enrollment in the regular class and stimulates his educational and emotional growth" (p. 14).

According to *The Resource Room,* Office of Programs for the Handicapped, South Carolina State Department of Education, "Resource programs can be an effective way of serving mildly handicapped children who are able to participate and function successfully for a portion of the school day in the regular educational program, but who require the diverse instructional modes which may be available to them in a resource room" (p. 1).

The resource room model becomes even more appropriate as

learning disabled students enter the middle and junior high schools where peer acceptance and conformity become the way of life. Here, being part of the mainstream of student activities is all-important. The use of the resource room model allows the student to receive needed remediation and personal support while maintaining his identity within the total school program.

The program model recommended in this manual is a resource room model serving mildly handicapped learning disabled students. The students are scheduled into the resource room for one period each day for remedial instruction in deficient areas. Help with homework assignments and preparation for regular classroom tests may also take place in the resource room. Students remain in regular classrooms for the majority of the day and participate in activities such as physical education, music, and art.

In addition to teaching students in the resource room, the resource teacher serves as a consultant to classroom teachers and helps plan the total educational program for the LD students.

As is true in the establishment of all new programs, the establishment of a resource room program should be preceded by thorough planning. If the program is to be effective, all those involved in the actual implementation should be included in the planning stages. Much greater cooperation is achieved if these people are involved in initial decision making and see a real need for the services to be provided.

Once school personnel decide that the resource room model is suitable to district needs, several things need to be considered. Among these are:

1. ARE ADEQUATE FACILITIES AVAILABLE? Although many a closet or supply room has been adequately converted for use as a resource room, this is not recommended. Neither is it necessary that a full-size classroom be used. What is essential is that the room has adequate lighting and ventilation and is large enough for the comfortable separation of students, so that small group and individual instruction do not interfere with other activities taking place in the room.

2. WHAT ABOUT COST? The cost of supplying a resource room may vary according to the amount of equipment already in the district that can be requisitioned to the resource room. A tape recorder, blank tapes, and earphones are a must. Occasional availability or the borrowing of this equipment from the school audiovisual library is not suitable, since this equipment is in use virtually every day, probably every period, including the teacher's planning period. Other equipment that is useful but not essential is a record player, an overhead projector, or a language master. Instructional materials, including curriculum kits and consumable materials, must also be purchased. Adequate funds, an estimated minimum of from eight hundred to one thousand dollars, must be made available if the resource room is to be properly equipped.

3. WHAT PERSONNEL WILL BE NECESSARY? In order to have an effective program for learning disabled students in the middle or junior high school, adequate staff must be available. In addition to the resource teacher, the school district should have a *full-time school psychologist* who evaluates students for placement in the resource room and serves as a member of the placement committee. The psychologist will also recommend program plans and remediation techniques and serve in the ongoing capacity of consultant to the resource teacher and parents. In some instances, he or she will also be called upon to provide counseling to the students.

Vision and *speech and hearing specialists* are needed for the initial screening of the LD students. These specialists will be available if the screening process warrants ongoing therapy or the need for referral to optometrists, ophthalmologists, and audiologists, etc.

The cooperation, understanding, and commitment of the building principal, guidance counselor, and regular classroom teachers are also essential components of a successful middle school program. The resource teacher alone cannot provide the support and success experiences necessary for the learning disabled student.

Principal support is necessary to provide an atmosphere of support, cooperation, and optimism among staff members. The support and commitment of classroom teachers cannot be over-emphasized. The regular classroom is where the LD student spends most of his or her school day. He or she is with students in his or her age-group who achieve success more readily than he or she. His or her success and acceptance in this classroom depend greatly on the acceptance and aid of the classroom teacher.

Guidance counselors should play a major role in the mainstreaming program. Hawisher and Calhoun (1978, p. 7) list the following examples of counselor involvement in a middle or junior high school program:

a. Meeting with resource students in small groups in order to familiarize the students with alternative methods of reactions in order that they may better deal with recurring problems of the school and home environment.
b. Aiding in the staff development program within the building in order to enhance the scholastic environment.
c. Meeting with parents to provide insight into the student's problems at school or at home.
d. Facilitating the scheduling of classes and study halls.
e. Bringing into the resource room and regular classroom counseling skills for better communication through the use of interviewing techniques.

Later sections deal with specific classroom teaching, guidance, and leadership strategies to promote effective mainstreaming.

Once plans have been made, preparation must be begun for the actual implementation of the program. Initial preparation should take place no later than the spring preceding the actual implementation year.

EMPLOYING A TEACHER

Probably the first step in preparation for the program should be the employment of a teacher who is certified by the state department of education in the area of learning disabilities. This is only the first of the qualifications needed by a teacher of learning disabled adolescents. In addition, this person should:

1. HAVE REGULAR CLASSROOM TEACHING EXPERIENCES: The demands placed upon a resource teacher if he or she is to work effectively within a middle school setting are great. This person must not only be able to work efficiently with students but must show that he or she is a valuable resource to teachers in the building. It is essential that the resource teacher is accepted by the faculty and staff as a worthwhile and contributing member. This can only be accomplished if the teacher is competent, understanding, and a real help to other teachers. He or she must have knowledge as to what is and is not a viable classroom activity for the LD student. This calls for a thorough understanding of the student, as well as alternatives for classroom instruction. The resource teacher must be willing to demonstrate teaching techniques, help gather necessary materials, and be available for consultation. Having been a regular classroom teacher, the resource teacher is better prepared to relate to the problems faced by these teachers in the classroom. Additionally, the more the resource teacher understands the needs and problems of the regular classroom, the more readily the teacher and the offered suggestions are accepted by the teachers in the school.

2. BE A SELF-DIRECTING PERSON: The effective management of a resource room is no easy task. The scheduling of students, parent conferences, teacher conferences, and placement committee meetings usually falls in the realm of resource teacher responsibility. In addition to scheduling requirements, classes must be well organized and lessons prepared for each student. In a middle school program, it is usually necessary to have from five to six students in the resource room at any given time. For fifty minutes, each of these students must be involved in worthwhile learning experiences, and often it is not feasible that any of these students work together on any one skill. The teacher's time and the students' activities must be organized and planned so that the teacher is able to spend a portion of the period in instructional time with each student. A teacher who is not self-directed and/or lacks organizational skills will be frustrated at the end of each day, and optimum learning will not have taken place.

3. SHOW COMPETENCE IN METHODS OF REMEDIAL INSTRUCTION: The primary responsibility of the resource teacher is the diagnosis and remediation of the learning problems presented by the learning disabled students. Competence in methods of remedial instruction is therefore of primary importance. The teacher must be able, through formal and informal assessment of student strengths and weaknesses, to determine what types of instruction are needed and what materials are best suited for this instruction. If the teacher is certified in the area of learning disabilities, he or she will have successfully completed a practicum experience with LD students. However, this experience may have been with younger students, and the teacher, therefore, will need to become acquainted with materials for this age-group. An important factor in material selection in the middle and junior high schools is the suitability to age level. There are many published materials today that are excellent for this age-group, and the successful resource teacher will become thoroughly familiar with these materials.

4. BE A PUBLIC RELATIONS PERSON: The resource teacher and the procedures of the resource room are highly visible to the building staff. Hawisher (1975) states that the success of the (resource room) program depends highly on the goodwill of principal, teachers, staff, pupils, and parents. This aspect of the program is extremely important and bears the same significance as teacher competency in educational skills. Hawisher (p. 9) lists the following hints for a resource teacher acting as a consultant to other staff members:

   a. Listen, hear, and understand what is being said by the regular classroom teacher.
   b. Acknowledge openly the skills held by the regular classroom teacher.
   c. Be cognizant of the problems faced by the regular classroom teacher.
   d. Adjust, or modify suggestions you may have, to the atmosphere of this particular regular classroom.
   e. Be honest.
   f. Seek the exchange of ideas and suggestions.

PREPARING THE ROOM

The preparation of the resource room may include the building of study carrels by students in the vocational school and moving furniture into or out of the room, etc. The resource room should be a pleasant, eye-appealing room, but it should be large enough so as not to look cluttered or overwhelming.

The resource room should contain several study carrels or other individual quiet areas where students can work without the interference and distractions of other activities. Work tables, student desks, and listening stations should be provided. The teacher will also need a filing cabinet for the systematic keeping of records and materials.

IDENTIFYING STUDENTS

Each year there will be LD students entering the middle or junior high school from feeder schools. Other students will have reached this school not yet identified as learning disabled. Steps must be taken to identify these students so that special services may be provided.

Cumulative records may be examined by the guidance counselor and/or resource teacher as a beginning step in the screening process. Things to be examined may include:

1. Scores on the *Comprehensive Tests of Basic Skills* or similar tests: Is the IQ score higher than achievement indicates? Are there highs and lows in areas of achievement?
2. Teacher comments through the years: Has the teacher said such things as "Johnny could do the work if he tried harder" or "Susie seems bright, but her reading achievement is very low."
3. Grades through the years: Has there been a consistent pattern of inconsistency?
4. Grades repeated: Did the child repeat one or more grades? If so, was there improvement in grades? What were the reasons for failure?
5. Special services: Has the student received special instruc-

Sample A

TEACHER REFERRAL FOR LD RESOURCE PROGRAM

Student's Name_____ Referring Teacher_____

Address_____

Sex_____ Age_____ Date of Birth_____

                                          Month   Day   Year

Parents _____

Grades Repeated_____

Estimate of Current Achievement Level

     Math_____ Reading_____ Spelling_____

Any Obvious Physical Handicaps_____

_____

Recent Test Data

Date	*Name of Test*	*Score-Results*

Reason for Referral

_____
_____
_____

What are the specific strengths (academic, behavioral) of this student?

1._____
2._____
3._____
4._____
5._____

What are the specific weaknesses (academic, behavioral) of this student?

1._____
2._____
3._____
4._____
5._____

What benefits do you feel that the resource room program would offer this student?

1._____
2._____
3._____
4._____
5._____

_____
Signature and position of referring person

_____
Principal's signature

Sample A *(continued)*
TEACHER REFERRAL FOR LD RESOURCE PROGRAM

For Resource Teacher Use _____

SIT Score_____ Date _____

WRAT Score   Reading_____ Math _____ Spelling _____ Date _____

Behavioral Observations_____

_____

Referred to Psychologist   Yes_____ No_____ Date_____

_____
Signature of Resource Teacher

tion in earlier grades? If so, what types of special services were provided, and what were the results?

The perusal of cumulative records often results in a substantial list of potential LD students. The guidance counselor, principal, or resource teacher should now confer with classroom teachers to get their impressions of the student as a possible candidate for resource room placement. If the teacher substantiates the need for further investigation, steps should be taken for individual screening and subsequent assessment by the school psychologist.

Teacher referrals may be solicited through in-service workshops. In addition to school personnel, those who may be made aware of available services and invited to make referrals should include:

Local physicians
Parents (through local newspapers, posters, etc.)
Local health departments
Mental health centers
Departments of social services

The referral form allows the referring person the opportunity to describe the degree to which the student possesses certain characteristics of the suspected learning disabled child. The referring person should state the specific reasons for the referral. The referral form aids the person responsible for screening and the school psychologist in recognizing the specific kind of student behavior exhibited in the classroom. A typical referral form is shown in Sample A.

Sample B

CONFIDENTIAL SOCIAL INFORMATION*

Date_____

Student's Name_____   Grade_____

Birthdate_____ Age_____ Sex _____ Race _____

Address_____   Telephone_____

Father's Name_____

Father's Occupation_____

Hours at Work_____

Highest grade completed in school_____

Mother's Name_____

Mother's Occupation_____

Hours at Work_____

Highest grade completed in school_____

Is either parent a stepparent?_____

Others Living in Home

Name	*Age*	*Relationship*
_____	_____	_____
_____	_____	_____
_____	_____	_____
_____	_____	_____

Birth weight of child_____

Was this child premature?_____

Were there any unusual circumstances or occurrences during pregnancy or birth?_____

_____

At what age did child walk?_____   Talk?_____

Has child ever been hospitalized?_____

Had serious high fever?_____

Convulsions?_____

Under treatment or medication at present?_____

Any other serious illnesses or accidents?_____

How would you rate your child's general health?_____

Do you think there are any family problems which may affect this child?_____

_____

Have other family members had difficulty in school?_____

_____

Sample B *(continued)*

Have other family members had emotional problems?_____
_____

What are your child's strengths?_____
_____

Weaknesses?_____
_____

What does your child do for fun?_____
_____

How does your child feel about school?_____

How do you feel about his program and/or progress?_____

What do you see as your child's biggest problem?_____

_____

* From South Carolina Region V Educational Services Center, 1975.

The referral form should be turned in to the building principal for his or her signature. He or she in turn gives the referral to the resource room teacher, who administers individual screening tests, including an academic aptitude (intelligence) test and an academic achievement test. Two tests that may be used are the *Slosson Intelligence Test* (SIT) and the *Wide Range Achievement Test* (WRAT). Classroom observations should also be made by the resource teacher, who should then record these observations along with the test data on the bottom portion of the referral form. If scores on the SIT are average or near average and scores on any portion of the WRAT are significantly below expectancy and/or other data suggests that the referral merits further steps, parental permission must be obtained for psychological evaluation.

A social history of the student to be placed in a learning disabilities program is needed at this time. The social history provides insights i: to the child's family background, medical history, and possible factors that may have contributed to the student's learning problems.

A parent conference conducted by the resource room teacher, ideally with the assistance of the school guidance counselor, is an excellent time to gather social history information and obtain written parent permission for the psychological evaluation. Rather than have the parent complete the social history form, the resource teacher should ask the questions and complete the form in an interview situation. In this way, more information may be gained, as answers may indicate further questions and areas of concern. Sample B is a social history form that may be used.

At this parent conference, the parents should be given information as to why a referral was made and the results of the screening process. They should also be advised of the possible services available for their son or daughter, whether or not special placement is warranted.

The resource teacher now has a folder containing the completed referral form, results of the screening evaluation (WRAT, SIT, and behavioral observations), the completed social history form, and parent permission for testing. This folder is given to the principal, who arranges with district personnel for the student evaluation.

EVALUATION FOR PLACEMENT

Regulations regarding specific learning disabilities as contained in the *Federal Register (42(250)*:65082-5, Dec. 29, 1977) specify that a multidisciplinary team shall be responsible for the evaluation of learning disabled students. This multidisciplinary team must include one of the student's regular teachers and a person qualified to conduct individual diagnostic examinations (remedial reading teacher, speech and language pathologist, or resource teacher). In most instances, the school psychologist administers an individual intelligence test. The child's performance in class must also be observed by someone other than the child's teacher.

A student is considered learning disabled if he or she (1) does not achieve commensurate with his or her age and ability when provided with appropriate educational experiences and (2) has a severe discrepancy between achievement and intellectual ability in one or more of the following seven areas:

1. Oral expression
2. Listening comprehension

Sample C
PLACEMENT FORM*

Learning Disabilities

Name_____   Age_____
        Last   First   Middle

Birthdate _____   _____

1. Vision within normal limits   Yes ____   No ____
2. Hearing within normal limits   Yes ____   No ____
3. No evidence of primary physical handicap_____
4. No evidence of primary emotional disturbance_____
5. No evidence of slow learner or environmental disadvantage_____
6. Current test battery results:

    a. Intelligence Test_____

    Date Administered_____

    Qualification of Examiner: Ed. Evaluator, Psy. 1, 2, or 3
                                               (Circle one)

    Score: Verbal_____ Performance_____ Full Scale_____

    b. Achievement Test _____

    Date Administered_____

    Name of Examiner_____ Position_____

    Percentile Score: Reading_____ Writing_____ Arithmetic___Spelling___

7. Date candidate must be re-evaluated_____
8. Has "procedural due process" been honored?   Yes ____   No ____
9. Diagnostic, evaluation, educational, and environmental data have been reviewed by a staffing committee, which recommends that the student is eligible for
   placement in a special program.

_____

(Specify model)

10. I certify that _____has met all criteria for
                                 Name

participation in a program for learning disabled pupils.

Signature_____

Person placing child in special program

Date of Placement _____

_____

* Adapted from the Office of Programs for the Handicapped, South Carolina Department of
  Education, 1976.

3. Written expression
4. Basic reading skills
5. Reading comprehension
6. Mathematics calculation
7. Mathematics reasoning

Referral, Screening, Evaluation, Placement

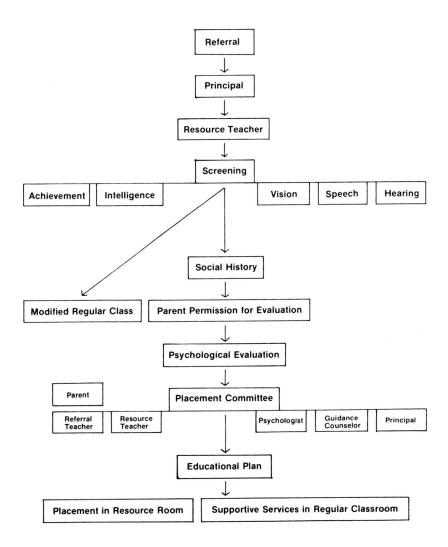

The *Federal Register* further states that the team may not identify a child as learning disabled if his learning problem is "primarily the result of (1) a visual, hearing, or motor handicap, (2) mental retardation, (3) emotional disturbance or (4)

environmental, cultural or economic disadvantage."

Upon the completion of the child's evaluation, which includes an intelligence measure, achievement tests, and observational reports, the evaluation team must prepare a written report, as outlined in the December 29, 1977, *Federal Register* (121a.543). Other pertinent data, such as the referral form, social history, and screening results, may be attached to this report.

PLACEMENT

The placement of a child into the learning disabilities resource room is the responsibility of a placement committee. One member of the evaluation team must be on the placement committee. Committee members for a middle school program might include:

1. Psychologist
2. Resource teacher
3. Guidance counselor
4. Principal
5. Classroom teacher
6. Parents
7. Student

Prior to final placement, individually sequenced instructional objectives should be developed for the student and kept on file by the resource teacher receiving the child.

If parents are unable to attend the placement meeting, results of the meeting must be communicated to them, and written permission for placement must be obtained. A placement form to be kept in the school is shown in Sample C and a diagram of the referral and screening process is also given.

PREPARING THE STAFF

In addition to being involved in the planning of the resource room program, teachers and other school personnel must be made aware, through in-service training, of the kinds of students to be served and of their role in the implementation of the program. Since the regular classroom teacher is the most likely person to make referrals for this program, he or she must know the kinds of things to look for before referral decisions are made. The first in-service program, held in the spring preceding the actual implementation year, may include discussions of the rationale behind the program, the services to be offered, and characteristics of LD students in general.

According to the South Carolina State Department of Education Procedures manual (1976): "In-service training sessions should be conducted by the local educational agency personnel responsible for special programs in an effort to apprise school personnel of the (1) existing special programs available to pupils who are handicapped, (2) the necessary referral procedures, (3) the functions/role of special education teachers, and (4) the legal responsibilities involved in the implementation and maintenance of special education programs." Suggested times for in-service sessions include:

1. Faculty meetings
2. District-wide orientation meetings
3. School board meetings
4. Principals' meetings

Teachers are more likely to accept the resource room program if they are made aware early of the benefits offered through the program. A handout and discussion of these services is beneficial.

The following services are available to the LD student and classroom teacher through the resource room program:

1. Diagnosis and remediation of the student learning problems.
2. Suggestions for curricular modifications to be used in the regular classroom.
3. Suggestions for materials and the loan of materials to be used in the regular classroom.
4. Suggestions for modifying student behavior in the classroom.
5. Help for students studying for tests or tutoring in skills necessary for fulfilling classroom assignments.
6. Taping lessons, etc., for use in the regular classroom.

The following checklist of adolescent learning disability characteristics may be given to teachers. Discussion and question and answer sessions should accompany this form.

LD Characteristics Sheet

1. A learning disabled student has average or above average intelligence.
2. A learning disabled student's learning problems are not primarily the result of visual, hearing or physical handicaps or mental retardation.

Any one or combinations of the following characteristics may be noted of a learning disabled student:

- Discrepancy in performance in academic areas
- Discrepancy between written and oral responses
- Reading level substantially below grade placement
- Difficulty in following directions
- Trouble in completing assignments
- Difficulty in attending to tasks
- Disorganization
- Problems in reasoning abstractly

- Poor spelling
- Poor handwriting
- Poor arithmetic skills
- Poor social skills

Further in-service sessions should deal with the proper completion of the referral form and referral procedures. Ongoing in-service formats are presented in Part III.

PART III

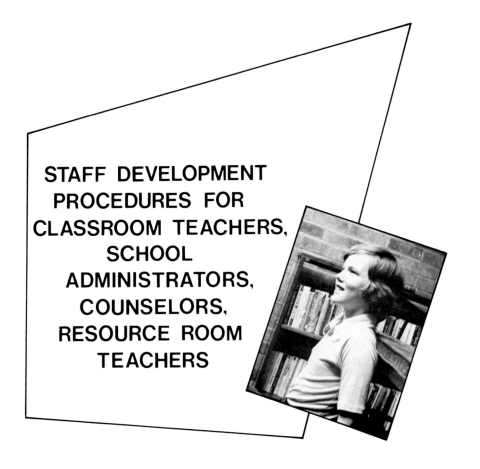

STAFF DEVELOPMENT
PROCEDURES FOR
CLASSROOM TEACHERS,
SCHOOL
ADMINISTRATORS,
COUNSELORS,
RESOURCE ROOM
TEACHERS

INTRODUCTION
TO THE
STAFF DEVELOPMENT COMPONENTS

THE LD adolescent's unique combination of learning problems, heretofore treated within the context of specialized classes, makes adaptation to the regular classroom environment extremely difficult. Nonindividualized classrooms, characterized by singular materials and singular instructional modes used in large group settings, do not promote the academic and social growth of LD students. Moving these students into the mainstream of the middle school's educational program requires organizational structures and instructional approaches that foster individualized teaching. This section presents one approach to assisting a school staff to develop such a program of individualized teaching, including suggested training procedures and materials that can be used as a basis for long-term total staff development.

Underlying Assumptions

The following are the assumptions or beliefs on which this approach to staff training is based. The assumptions can be used as a guiding force to give direction to the development of training activities and as a set of performance criteria to help judge the effectiveness of activity implementation:

1. STAFF DEVELOPMENT ACTIVITIES SHOULD INVOLVE THE ENTIRE STAFF — PRINCIPAL COUNSELORS, AND TEACHERS. Both administrative and instructional adjustments must be made in promoting personalized instruction for LD students; students may need considerable counseling in making the transition from specialized to regular classes. Academic success and social adjustment for the LD student are enhanced to the extent that the total staff is concerned, informed, and committed to the student's growth and development.

2. STAFF DEVELOPMENT ACTIVITIES SHOULD BE AS REALITY ORIENTED AS POSSIBLE. All training activities should occur in the school and in classrooms, the only places where the effectiveness of new instructional approaches can be verified.

3. STAFF DEVELOPMENT ACTIVITIES SHOULD BE PERFORMANCE BASED. Activities should extend beyond an awareness or knowledge level to provide staff members actual practice in making instructional adjustments and in implementing new individualized techniques.

4. STAFF DEVELOPMENT ACTIVITIES SHOULD BE MONITORED CAREFULLY, PROVIDING FEEDBACK TO PARTICIPANTS. As staff members are learning new behaviors and techniques for teaching LD students, they need frequent feedback regarding the quality of their efforts and the extent to which their methods will provide for the special needs of LD students.

5. STAFF DEVELOPMENT ACTIVITIES SHOULD FOSTER STAFF CREATIVITY AND FLEXIBILITY. While staff members need sufficient structure to guide their learning, they also need maximum opportunity within that structure to generate new and different ideas for teaching LD students.

6. STAFF DEVELOPMENT ACTIVITIES SHOULD BE SELF-ADMINISTERED. School staffs are capable of conducting their own training with a minimum of outside consultant help, provided they have capable in-school leadership and some structured procedures to follow.

7. STAFF DEVELOPMENT SHOULD PROVIDE PRACTICAL "PAYOFFS" FOR PARTICIPANTS, PARTICULARLY FOR CLASSROOM TEACHERS. Commitment for long-term staff development can be gained from those involved only if they can clearly see the

implication of training activities for meeting instructional needs in the classroom. Training activities should provide for practical and immediate application of newly acquired knowledge and skills that will yield positive results, not only with LD students but also with other students in the classroom.

Staff Development Components

The program of staff development, designed in terms of the above assumptions, is organized into four separate but overlapping interdependent training components (Fig. 1). Components are (1) classroom teaching, (2) resource room teaching, (3) counseling, and (4) instructional leadership.

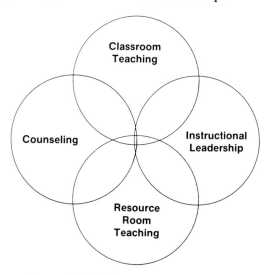

Figure 1. Staff development components.

Although any one of these training components can be implemented independently, a total staff approach, in which all components are implemented concurrently, is recommended. Many of the training activities, particularly at an awareness level, are similar for all components and can be used to bring administrative, teaching, and counseling personnel together in a common focus. In addition, it is recommended that staff members be involved in the various training components, as shown in Figure 2. This does not mean that all staff members participate in all training activities in each component designated for them. Involvement in other components is intended to build an awareness of other staff roles, which is necessary to fulfilling primary functions. That all staff members are involved, at least in part, in the classroom component, emphasizes the importance of total staff awareness of the classroom function in providing successful mainstreaming.

Component	Classroom Teachers	Resource Teachers	Counselor	Principal
1. Classroom Teaching	X*	X	X	X
2. Resource Room Teaching		X*		
3. Counseling		X	X*	
4. Leadership Training	X	X*	X	X

* Indicates primary training.

Figure 2. Staff involvement in staff development components.

The staff development components presented in Part III are intended to be used as self-instructional training sequences administered by an instructional leader in the school. The LD resource teacher is perhaps the most logical source of leadership, providing this person possesses some knowledge of curriculum organization, instructional processes, and supervision. If not, the leadership function can be assumed by the school's principal, curriculum coordinator, master teacher, or counselor. In any case, it is assumed that the LD resource teacher has sufficient expertise in learning disabilities to serve as the content resource person for the school.

Each of the training sequences that follows is written specifically for staff development leaders. The procedures, activities, and materials included are intended to provide a framework for training and not a "cookbook" to be dogmatically followed.

Parts of a sequence may be adapted to a self-pacing format for staff members to work on individually; other parts may lend themselves better to small group work. The staff development leader in the school is encouraged to use the ideas and materials presented to generate additional activities and materials designed to achieve training objectives.

COMPONENT 1.

TRAINING SEQUENCE FOR CLASSROOM TEACHING

A Message to Staff Development Leaders

Teaching learning disabled students in middle school classrooms with twenty, twenty-five, or thirty-five other students, each with his or her own special learning strengths and weaknesses, is no simple task. It requires first an awareness of the general characteristics of LD adolescents and then, in particular, an awareness of the learning styles, interests, and abilities of students in the school. In addition, teaching LD adolescents requires an ability to make specific adjustments in instruction, adjusting ways in which teachers use time, space, materials, etc. Finally, successful instruction for LD adolescents involves an ability to incorporate specific instructional adjustments into individualized instructional techniques, such as contracts, learning packages, and learning centers.

These areas of concern, creating *awareness,* making *instructional adjustments,* and developing *instructional techniques,* constitute three levels of staff development in this training sequence (Fig. 3).

Level 1 — Awareness Training

Objective: After completing this level of training, school staff members will be able to describe the general characteristics of LD adolescents and the particular learning problems of the LD students they teach.

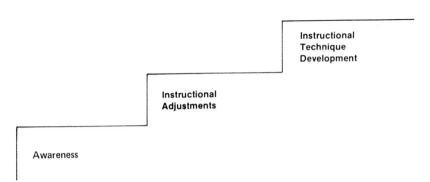

Figure 3. Classroom training three levels of teaching.

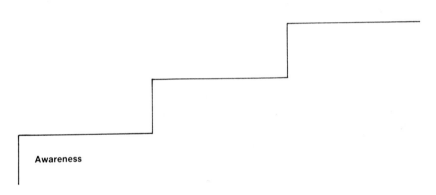

Awareness Experiences

It is difficult, if not impossible, for regular classroom teachers to work effectively with LD students if they are only vaguely aware of their learning problems.

The staff development leader cannot assume that school staff members have this awareness or that they are sensitive to the needs of LD adolescents. The leader also cannot assume that an occasional handout list of LD characteristics or periodic notes from the resource teacher will foster teacher awareness of and commitment to the LD student. The level of teacher commitment to helping LD youngsters compensate for their disabilities in the various subject areas depends greatly on the level of staff awareness. Therefore, what is needed is a variety of awareness experiences providing school staff members with frequent long-term opportunities for examining the characteristics and learning problems of their LD students.

The following awareness activities are suggested as examples of training experiences for building teacher awareness. It is recommended that some of the activities be used in initial training sessions, while others be used as reinforcement during the training year:

1. *Films and filmstrips followed by discussion* are good introductory activities for building awareness of the general characteristics of LD adolescents. Follow the film or filmstrip with such questions as, "Who are the students you have who seem to exhibit behaviors similar to those shown in the film?" "What are the behaviors of your students that would identify them as LD?" "What are behaviors of these students that seem inconsistent with LD identification?" Two films that are excellent for introductory training and which provide good possibilities for follow-up discussion are: (1) *A Walk in Another Pair of Shoes,* which is narrated by Tennessee Ernie Ford. Viewers follow Mark, a learning disabled youngster, through a typical school day. The filmstrip, by having viewers experience visual and auditory perceptual difficulties, leaves them with an understanding of what it means to be learning disabled. The filmstrip shows that LD students can be highly successful learners. (2) *Adolescents and Learning Disabilities* depicts the obstacles learning disabled adolescents face as they struggle for educational, social, and economic survival in modern society. The film suggests ways in which adults can help these youngsters to participate more successfully both within and outside the school.

2. An excellent method for giving training participants a feeling for what it is like to be learning disabled is to involve them in short *simulated exercises.* For example, tracing mirror images helps teachers experience and analyze feelings and behaviors that emerge from failing at a simple task. A good resource for exercises such as these is *Oh, Dear, Somebody Said "Learning Disabilities"! A Book for Teachers and Parents* (Hayes, 1975).

3. Short and simple *articles* written in nontechnical language are a quick way to build teacher awareness of general

characteristics of LD students. Articles written for parents can be particularly good for communicating essential but nontechnical information to school staff members. Ten-minute reading periods followed by brief reaction and discussion periods seem to be effective. Several recommended sources are:

- "A Parent's Guide to Learning Disabilities," *Today's Health* (Sept. 1975).

- Although extensive reading in texts on learning disabilities does *not* appear to be critical to school staff awareness, there is one book that seems superior to others in its clarity and simplicity. *The Educator's Enigma: The Adolescent With Learning Disabilities* (Schloss, 1971) is about fifty pages long and can be used in part or in its entirety by school staff members.

4. One method of focusing school staff attention on printed information and/or of determining the extent of acquired knowledge about LD adolescents is to have training participants construct *collages* symbolizing their concept of "who is the LD adolescent." Collages or drawings can be done individually or in groups. They can be presented and their meanings discussed. Misconceptions about LD adolescents are often revealed through this activity. Collages can be done early in a training session, put on display, and modified as staff awareness broadens and deepens.

5. *Role playing* periodically during training sessions is another creative means of building awareness and determining the depth of staff knowledge. Role plays can be structured for training participants around typical difficulties that the LD adolescent might encounter in relationships with teachers, school administrators, peers, parents, and other adults outside the school setting. Appropriate and inappropriate adult responses to LD behavior can be displayed and analyzed. Several suggested role play situations are:

   a. Science teacher confronts LD student with consistent failure to complete assignments.

   b. LD adolescents who cannot read must obtain a bottle of aspirin from drug store; interacts with clerk.

   c. School principal confronts LD adolescent with his consistent misbehavior in social studies class.

An excellent resource for teaching the role-playing process is *Role-Playing Methods in the Classroom* (Chesler and Fox, 1966).

6. Perhaps the most important facet of awareness for staff members is the understanding of the specific learning problems of LD students within their own school and classrooms. This awareness can be acquired in several ways:

a. When the student has been properly identified by the school system as learning disabled, school staff members can *observe* him or her carefully in terms of their general knowledge about LD adolescents.

STUDENT PROFILE

Name_____*Sam*_____ C.A._____12-6_____ Date_____

A. Test Results:

SIT

M.A._____12-3_____ IQ____98____

WRAT

Spelling____2.9____ Math____7.0____   Reading____4.2____

PIAT

Math____7.6____ Reading Recog.____4.0____   Reading Comp.____4.8____

Spelling____3.4____ General Info.____7.6____ Total____4.8____

B. Weakness

1. Inability to read grade level texts
2. Inability to follow more than one direction at a time
3. Inability to express himself because of illegible cursive writing and poor spelling
4. Inability to perform manipulative skills because of poor coordination

C. Strengths

1. Good rote memory skills in basic arithmetic operations and simple sight words
2. Good attention span
3. Good verbal skills
4. Good general knowledge of science and social studies concepts

D. Specific Areas of Needed Remediation

1. Cursive writing
2. Spelling
3. Reading comprehension skills
4. Following directions
5. Sequencing (historical data, sentence structure, etc.)

Figure 4.

b. The resource teacher within the school can provide teachers with a *profile* of the strengths and weaknesses of LD students in each teacher's class. Profiles should be "teacher oriented." Strengths and weaknesses listed should include only those relevant to student performance in the particular subject matter areas and should be stated in nontechnical language. A sample profile developed by a resource teacher for classroom teachers is shown in Figure 4.

c. Short but frequent *conferences* between the resource teacher and the classroom teacher help teachers gain awareness of their own LD students. The principal and counselor can also be participants in conferences. Conferences can be used to discuss and interpret student profiles. Classroom teachers and the resource teacher can share insights about students not included on profiles, discuss student progress, and add new observations and insights to profiles during the year. Conferences need not last longer than ten minutes, but should be held as frequently as once per week, if possible.

Summary

Awareness training for school staff members should focus on creating understanding of the general characteristics of LD adolescents through films, filmstrips, short articles, simulated activities, and creative experiences such as collages and role playing. Training should also focus on creating staff awareness of the particular learning problems of the LD students in their own school and classrooms through observation, distribution of student profiles, and through short conferences between the resource teacher and other staff members.

Level 2 — Instructional Adjustments

Objectives: After completing this level of training, school staff members will be able to make specific *instructional adjustments* to assist LD students in compensating for their learning problems.

Instructional
Adjustments

Awareness

Instructional Adjustment Training

Awareness of the learning problems of LD adolescents is a critical prerequisite to providing for these students instructionally in the classroom. However, awareness in itself by no means implies that teachers will be able to make the necessary adjustments in their instruction. Developing appropriate instructional adjustments for LD students is a learned process, and school staff members need procedures for helping them to learn to make sound decisions, to practice new instructional approaches, and to reflect on the quality of their efforts.

The purpose of training at this level is not to confront the staff member with procedures for redesigning the school curricula. Rather, the focus is one of helping teachers learn to make special provisions for LD students within the existing instructional program, to help them compensate for their deficiencies.

Compensation for learning deficiencies in the various subject areas, not remediation of these deficiencies, is the instructional priority in the mainstreaming approach. The following is a five-step process for helping school staff members insure LD student success through simple instructional adjustments:

Step 1.
*What will
student
be required
to do?
What
obstacles
may prevent
him from
doing it?*

- Begin by having teachers identify the activities they have planned for their students in some lesson they will actually be teaching. Have them identify the performance students will be expected to demonstrate and materials they will be expected to use.

- Then, have teachers refer to the profile of one of their LD students (*see* Fig. 4) and anticipate the specific learning problems or obstacles the LD student will face in performing the planned activities. For initial training purposes, it may be helpful to provide a hypothetical lesson and/or profile and have participants compare anticipated learning problems based on the same information. This should give each participant opportunity for feedback regarding the appropriateness of his or her individual conclusions, as compared to other staff members. The accuracy of anticipated learning problems can be judged in terms of the consistency between what the student will be required to do and the student's specific disabilities. Form A provides sample documentation of information in Step 1. Appendix A includes a blank copy of this form (and those that follow) that may be cut out and photocopied for use with teachers.

Step 2.
*Adjust one
instruc-
tional
variable.*

- Given the anticipated learning obstacles, hypothetical or real, that the LD student may encounter in performing the planned class activities successfully, it is possible for subject teachers to adjust a number of variables in class activities to help the LD student compensate for his or her deficiencies. Teachers have control of, and can manipulate, the following in-

Form A

LD Student
LEARNING PROBLEM IDENTIFICATION

Student_____*Sam*_____ Teacher/Subject___*Jones/Math*

1. State what it is that students in the class will be doing. What *activities* will they be engaged in? What *materials* will they be expected to use? What *performance* will they be expected to demonstrate?

   • Using a series of worksheets, students will practice multiplication of whole numbers by simple fractions.

   • Each worksheet will consist of fifteen examples and five word problems.

   • Students are required to do one worksheet each day. Textbooks can be used as a resource and the teacher will provide individual help.

2. Based on your observations, judgement, and information from the resource teacher, what do you anticipate will be the *learning problems* or *obstacles* the LD student will face in achieving this knowledge or skill?

   a. Student works slowly, may become discouraged by number of problems on worksheet, and may have trouble focusing attention on each problem.

   b. Student's reading problems may make it difficult for him to understand the intent of word problems.

3. Is the above list of anticipated *learning problems* logically derived from the student's specific disabilities in terms of the performance he or she will have to demonstrate?   Yes _X_   No ___

Comment: *J. Smith*

                                 Staff Development Leader

Blank form in Appendix A.

structional variables:
   Time
   Space
   Material
      Amount
      Sequence
      Difficulty
      Type
   Grouping
   Mode of presentation and evaluation
Examples of ways in which each of these variables can be adjusted for LD students are found in Appendix B.
• Give teachers the suggested list of adjustments organized around each of the instructional vari-

ables (Appendix B) and have them select *one* adjustment to alleviate one of the learning problems listed in Step 1. If a hypothetical problem is used, one adjustment could be selected by the total participating group, by several subgroups, or individually, so that alternatives could be compared. The appropriateness of adjustment selection can be analyzed and judged in terms of the consistency between the identified learning problem and the probability that the adjustment will alleviate the problem.

- After selection and description of an appropriate adjustment on Form B, have teachers consider and list on the form the way(s) they will evaluate the effectiveness of the adjustment.
- As school staff members begin planning adjustments for actual implementation with LD students, they should begin with *one* adjustment for *one* learning problem. Planning multiple adjustments can initially distract attention from the need to make quality selections that

assure success. In addition, it is difficult to assess the effectiveness of any one adjustment if it is combined with others. Teachers seem to be more accepting of and progress faster in this approach if they plan and implement in the beginning a simple adjustment that works.

Form B
LD Student
INSTRUCTIONAL ADJUSTMENT

Student_____*Sam*_____ Teacher/Subject_____*Jones/Math*_____

1. Describe *instructional adjustment(s)* devised to compensate for anticipated learning problems, to enhance learning of LD student. Tell what you intend to do, how you intend to do it, and how you expect your adjustments to meet the needs of the LD student.

   a. I will cut worksheets into sections of two problems each, having Sam work on one section at a time until he completes the entire worksheet. Depending on the student's work speed, I may slightly reduce the number of examples and problems on each worksheet.

   b. I will have Sam choose another student to serve as a reader to help him understand directions and the meaning of word problems. The reader will help only when the LD student considers it necessary.

2. Describe how you will *evaluate* the effectiveness of your instructional adjustment.

   a. I will keep an account of the number of problems Sam completes each day, noting increases and decreases.

   b. I will observe Sam to determine the length of time he can work efficiently.

   c. I will ask Sam to help me assess how he is doing each day.

---

3. Does there seem to be consistency between the instructional adjustment(s) recommended above and the anticipated learning problems identified in Step 1 (Form A)?   Yes _*X*_   No ___

Comment: *J. Smith*
                              Staff Development Leader
   Blank form in Appendix A.

Step 3.
Implement and evaluate the adjustment.

• Once an initial adjustment is planned, staff members should "try it out" in the classroom with the LD student for whom the adjustment is intended. The length of the implementation depends entirely on the nature of the adjustment, but, in all cases, sufficient time should be allotted to fairly test the approach. For example, the math teacher who adjusts the amount of material by giving the LD student one multiplication problem at a time until he completes required assignments should use this adjustment for at least a week before deciding whether it is or is not effective.

- It is important that staff members critically evaluate the successes and/or failures of adjustments. There can be much "throwing out the baby with the bath water" in assessment of instructional adjustments for students. Teachers may react to the failure of an adjustment by assuming that the particular adjustment, or any other adjustment, will not work with any LD student. Closer examination of the adjustment may reveal that it failed because of the *way* in which it was implemented, because *timing* of its use was poor, or because the student misunderstood its *purpose*.

- Form C can be used for evaluating adjustments. Completing the form, particularly for initial adjustments, focuses teacher attention on specific evidence of and reasons for successes and failures. Follow-up sessions should also be held to allow each staff member opportunities to share successes and failures with other staff members. Follow-up sharing can be done with the total staff, in small staff subgroups, or in one-to-one conferences with the staff development leader. Follow-up dialogue among staff members can help participants clarify their thinking about the effectiveness of their adjustments.

Step 4.
Plan and
implement
multiple
adjustments.

- As staff members begin to feel comfortable and successful with planning, implementing, and evaluating singular adjustments, they can gradually move toward using multiple adjustments to further enhance LD student achievement.

Form C

EVALUATION OF INSTRUCTIONAL ADJUSTMENT

Student_____*Sam*_____ Teacher/Subject____*Jones/Math*____

1. What evidence do you have that the student did (or did not) benefit from the adjustment(s)? Attach results of tests or questionnaires.

Objective Evidence

Sam was able each day to complete an average of twelve of the fifteen examples and three of the five word problems. Previously, he was completing only five or six items on the worksheet.

Subjective Evidence

Sam seems to be happier in class, appears to be less anxious about his work, and is proud of the number of examples and problems he is completing.

2. How do you account for the success or failure of the adjustment(s)? To what extent were you able to implement the adjustment(s) as you planned?

I found in the beginning that I had to reduce the number of problems in each section to *one* to keep Sam working efficiently. However, after several days, I was able to increase the number of examples and problems to two and eventually to three.

3. What additional adjustments would you consider making to enhance the performance of the LD student?

a. I plan to section Sam's next test, giving him one problem at a time.

Notes:

Blank form in Appendix A.

- However, there is no recommended time schedule for increasing the number of students involved or for increasing the number of adjustments per student. Some teachers are ready to plan multiple adjustments for LD students after only one or two singular adjustments, while others need repeated practice extending over several months.
- Growth in use of adjustments generally consists of planning one adjustment around several learning problems for one student; gradually increasing the number of adjustments for each particular learning problem of a student; periodically planning adjustments for

additional students; and finally planning and implementing multiple adjustments for the learning problems of every LD student in the class. A general recommended time frame for the planning of an initial adjustment for one student to incorporation of multiple adjustments for all LD students in the school is four to six months.

Step 5. *Adjustment profile for each student.*

• The final step in training staff members to adjust instructional variables for LD students is to encourage each teacher to maintain a profile of the adjustments made for each LD student during the year. Form D is provided for this purpose. Maintenance of the adjustment profiles gives a continuous accounting of the

Form D
INSTRUCTIONAL ADJUSTMENT
SUMMARY SHEET

Student Name_____*Sam*_____ Subject_____*Math*_____

Performance Problems	Instructional Adjustments	Outcomes
1. Difficulty focusing attention on multiple tasks, such as a sheet containing twenty math problems.	1. Sequence tasks in limited numbers; i.e. give one or two math problems at a time.	1. Can complete nearly all tasks assigned.
2. Difficulty in understanding written directions and word problems.	2. Use peer helper as a reading resource person.	2. Sam accepts and utilizes peer helper as needed. Follows directions more accurately and successfully completes word problems.
3. Etc.		

Notes:

Blank form in Appendix A.

student's performance problems identified during the year; the specified instructional adjustments used to overcome each problem; and the extent to which the adjustments have been successful (outcomes). Adjustment profiles can be useful as a resource of suggested adjustments to be used for students with similar problems and as baseline information for adapting instruction for the student as he or she moves from teacher to teacher.

Summary

Instructional adjustment training for school staff members comprises a five-step sequence designed to help teachers assist LD students in compensating for their learning deficiencies within the existing instructional program. The five teaching steps include:

1. Determining what the students will be required to do in class; what performances they are expected to demonstrate; and what obstacles may prevent the LD student from performing successfully.
2. Planning to adjust one instructional variable for one student to help the LD student overcome one of the obstacles listed in Step 1.
3. Implementing and evaluating the effectiveness of the adjustment planned in Step 2.
4. Planning, implementing, and evaluating multiple adjustments for each LD student in the class.

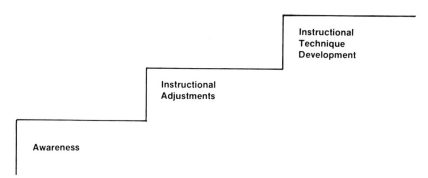

5. Maintaining a profile of the adjustments made for each LD student during the year.

Additional documented samples of this procedure are presented in Appendix C.

Level 3 — Instructional Technique Development

OBJECTIVE: School staff members will be able to incorporate specific instructional adjustments for LD students into structured teaching techniques, such as contracts, unit lesson plans, learning centers, and learning packages.

Instructional Development Training

The third level of training is designed to help school staff members learn to build multiple adjustments for LD students into unit lesson plans and into individualized techniques, such as contracts, learning packages, and learning centers. Training at this level encourages staff members to go beyond making short-range adjustments for students to more systematic long-range planning.

Some teachers, particularly those who are highly textbook oriented and most comfortable with group-paced instruction, will have difficulty adapting to this level of training. The staff development leader may even decide to omit these teachers from participation, encouraging them to continue to make adjustments for LD students in their daily lessons. However, teachers who normally tend to individualize instruction will find that they can more systematically help LD adolescents overcome their learning difficulties by incorporating adjustments into individualized teaching techniques.

The following is a four-step procedure intended to guide staff participants in developing individualized approaches for middle school LD students in all academic subject areas:

Step 1. • Have each staff member begin by developing,
Develop   in his subject area, a short learning contract for
learning   one LD student. Contracts can be developed
contract   around a common hypothetical student profile

with adjust-
ments for LD
students.

such as the one presented on page 38 or for an actual LD student in each teacher's class. Use of the hypothetical profile allows participants to assess the quality of their contracts in comparison to others. Contract development for an actual student provides realism and practicality to the process.

- The contract is suggested as a beginning point because it is relatively easy to construct and can be accomplished in a short period of time.

- It is not the intention of this procedure to recommend particular formats for developing contracts or any other of the instructional approaches. Rather, the procedure seeks to insure adaptation of any technique to the particular problems of LD students. Several resources that seem to offer adequate guidance in the development of contracts and other individualized approaches are —
  - *One at a Time All at Once* (Blackburn and Powell, 1976).
  - *Practical Approaches to Individualizing Instruction,* (Dunn and Dunn, 1972).
  - *Preparing and Using Individualized Learning Packages for Ungraded Continuous Progress Education* (Kapfer and Ovard, 1971).
  - *Invitation to Learning: The Learning Center Handbook* (Voight, 1971).

- Figure 5 presents a list of *adaptation criteria* to guide staff members in their development of contracts for LD students. In addition, sample contracts (constructed for the student profile shown on page 38) are included in Appendix D.

- It is recommended that initial contracts be kept short and that they include no more than two or three adjustments. A contract designed for

CONTRACTS FOR LD STUDENTS
ADAPTATION CRITERIA

1. The contract should reflect adjustments for the particular needs of LD students as described in your student profile.
2. The contract should contain simple explicit instructions to the student about what he is to do.
3. The contract should include a simply worded statement of purpose (objective) of the contract; several activities designed to achieve the purpose; and evaluation procedures to determine the extent to which the purpose has been met.
4. Learning activities should be detailed, fully explaining what the student and the teacher will do; what materials will be used; how materials will be used, etc.
5. Learning activities should contain limited content, reflect limited amounts of time, and provide for immediate feedback.
6. Materials suggested should be either easily accessible to the student or should be developed and included with the contract.
7. Learning activities should reflect variety in modality but should emphasize the LD student's modality strengths.
8. All student materials should contain simple, precise language. Amount of information on a page should be limited.
9. Curriculum materials included should be as creative and attractive as possible.

Figure 5.

Step 2.
Review and revise contracts in terms of adaptation criteria.

one class period or shorter is sufficient.
• After the initial development of the contracts, staff members should have an opportunity for feedback on the quality of their efforts. Constructive feedback can be provided through a critique of the contracts by the staff development leader within the school or by the teachers themselves. Perhaps the more valuable learning experience for staff members is to have them exchange contracts and criticize them carefully, using the list of adaptation criteria (Fig. 5) as a review guide. Staff members can then share their critiques on a one-to-one basis, revising their initial work as necessary.

Step 3.
Implement

• After staff members have developed, critiqued, and revised contracts, they are ready to use

*and
evaluate
contract.*

them with LD students in their classrooms. If hypothetical contracts were developed in Step 1, real contracts, incorporating actual adjustments for LD students in their classes, should be developed and revised as needed before implementation.

- It is important that teachers carefully evaluate the effectiveness of their *contracts* with students as they did with their *adjustments* in training Level 2, Step 3. Unsuccessful contracts in particular should be analyzed to determine the reason(s) for failure. Evaluation of contracts encourages staff members to be analytical about the quality of their instruction and avoids abandonment of promising practices with LD students because of initial failure.

- Form E can be used for evaluating contract implementation. Completing the form focuses teacher attention on specific evidence of and reasons for successes and failures of contracts. Follow-up sharing of the outcomes of contract implementation can be done with the total staff, in small subgroups or in one-to-one conferences with a staff development leader. Follow-up dialogue among staff members can help them clarify their thinking about the effectiveness of their contracts.

Step 4.
*Adapt
additional
instructional
techniques to
the needs of
LD students.*

- As staff members become proficient at developing contracts for LD students, they should have little difficulty with adapting other instructional techniques, such as instructional units, learning packages, centers, games, and small group learning to the needs of LD students. The same training procedures used for contract development (Fig. 5) and implementation (Form E) are also applicable to these other techniques. The staff leadership can determine the extent to which formalized training procedures are necessary to assist staff members in incorporating instructional adjustments into the other approaches. However, the procedures of shared planning and evaluation described in Steps 1 through 3 are recommended as a continuing process for achieving high-quality instruction for LD students.

- A sample learning package and learning center descriptions, adapted to the needs of the LD student profiled on page 38, are presented in Appendix E.

Form E
EVALUATION OF CONTRACT IMPLEMENTATION

1. What evidence do you have that the student did (or did not) benefit from the contract? Attach student work, results of test, or questionnaires.

    Objective Evidence

    Subjective Evidence

2. How do you account for the success or failure of the contract? How did the inclusion of each adjustment in the contract contribute to the student's success (or failure)?

3. What additional adjustments would you consider making in your next contract to enhance the performance of the LD student?

Summary

Instructional technique development training for school staff members consists of a four-step sequence designed to help teachers incorporate specific instructional adjustments for LD students into structured teaching techniques such as contracts, unit lesson plans, learning centers, and learning packages. The four training steps include:

1. Developing a contract for an LD student, incorporating instructional variable adjustments to help the LD student overcome his learning difficulties.

2. Reviewing and revising the contract in terms of specific adaptation criteria.

3. Implementing and evaluating the effectiveness of the contract developed in Steps 1 and 2.
4. Incorporating instructional adjustments into additional techniques such as unit lesson plans and learning packages.

The Learning Environment

Adjusting the variables of instruction for LD students in the regular classroom may cause resentment among students who view the adjustments as "special treatment." The potential for student resentment can be present in any classroom where the teacher attempts to personalize instruction. It is even more likely to occur in classrooms where teachers employ primarily nonindividualized instruction and then begin to make individual adjustments for LD students. It is important that all staff members be aware that these negative feelings can arise and learn to take positive steps to prevent them.

Maintaining effective instruction for LD students in the regular classroom requires that the teacher provides from the first class period an atmosphere of acceptance of individual differences and commitment to mutual helping and support. It is important that every student in the class not only accepts the fact that LD students, as well as their other classmates, possess certain learning strengths and weaknesses, but that they also become open to both giving and receiving help when it is needed.

One way for teachers to establish a classroom atmosphere in which students accept and support adjusting instruction for LD students is by openly and honestly discussing with them the fact that they all have different learning strengths and weaknesses and can expect to be taught in different ways during the year. In some classes, this is sufficient to establish tolerance for personalizing instruction for LD students. However, an even deeper student appreciation of individual differences and commitment to helping LD students succeed can be achieved if the teacher conducts, during the year, a series of activities focused on accepting differences in oneself and others.

Teachers may need guidance from the staff development leader in selecting the most appropriate activities for building self-acceptance of others in the classroom. Each of the following sources is recommended because it contains many practical and easy-to-administer activities for middle and junior high school students:

- *The Other Side of the Report Card: A How-to-Do-It Program for Affective Education* (Chase, 1975).
- *One Hundred Ways to Enhance Self-Concept in the Classroom* (Canfield and Wells, 1976).
- *Kids Accepted Here: Activities for the Classroom* (Drew, 1975). This is oriented to elementary but easily adaptable to middle school youngsters.
- *Values Clarification: A Handbook of Practical Strategies for Teachers and Students* (Simon, Howe, and Kirschenbaum, 1972).

COMPONENT 2.
RESOURCE TEACHER TRAINING SEQUENCE
A Message to Staff Development Leaders

The resource room teacher has been trained to remediate the learning problems of learning disabled students. He or she has a wealth of knowledge about the characteristics of learning disabled students and methods of instruction to be used in the resource room. However, it cannot be assumed that the resource teacher has been trained, or is aware of, the vast amount of record keeping that is required in the operation of a resource room. Neither can it be assumed that the resource teacher is aware of the importance of teacher contacts, parent contacts, and the overall cooperative effort of all staff members for the effective mainstreaming of middle school learning disabled students.

Too often, the resource teacher is set apart from the other faculty members, with little interaction between resource teacher and classroom teachers. If there are several special teachers in a building, they tend to band together, socially and professionally. Classroom teachers have little opportunity to know exactly what it is that goes on behind the closed doors of the "resource room." They know only that some of their students go there for special help during the school day and are still unable to do the work required in their classroom.

The purposes of the training procedures that follow are to help resource teachers keep accurate and beneficial records and to become competent in interactions with other school personnel and parents in providing a system of feedback and communication.

Training Procedures

OBJECTIVES: After completing this training sequence, resource teachers will be able to communicate effectively with classroom teachers concerning LD students.

Awareness Experiences

Since resource teachers have extensive knowledge and training in the area of learning disabilities, awareness training for them takes a different focus than awareness training for regular teachers, counselors, and staff development leaders. One area in which awareness training may be needed is the school curriculum for the students they teach. To be able to communicate effectively with teachers and make meaningful suggestions for classroom adjustments, the resource teacher should be familiar with the textbooks used in the school and also the particular teaching styles of the teachers in the building. Only through knowledge in these areas will the resource teacher be able to make suggestions for classroom instruction that he or she is reasonably sure will work. In addition, he or she will be better prepared to help learning disabled students with their regular classroom assignments, something meaningful and important to a middle school student in the mainstream of education.

The following activities are suggested to help resource teachers become acquainted with the school curriculum:

1. *Get copies* of all science, social studies, English, and math textbooks used by the learning disabled students in the resource room. Go through the books. Look at and make a copy of the table of contents and then look through the books to see what is covered under each topic. Look at the vocabulary. Determine what difficulties the LD students will have with the text. Determine what can be done in the resource room and regular classroom to alleviate or lessen some of these problems.

2. *Get into conversations* with teachers about their classes and the kinds of instructional techniques they use, etc. Talk to them about what the LD student does in the classroom, how he or she performs. Much information can be gained in this way, i.e. whether the LD student is expected to do the same things the other students are expected to do and whether the textbook is used extensively, etc.

3. *Classroom observations* are invaluable to the resource teacher, and several observations should be made before the student is scheduled into the resource room. By going into the classroom to see what kinds of problems are encountered by the LD student and how he or she reacts to different classroom situations, the resource teacher can again get insights into teaching styles, how the teacher reacts to the LD student, and how the student reacts to the teacher, and what kinds of suggestions have possibilities for working in a particular classroom.

Summary

Awareness training for resource teachers should be directed toward a good general knowledge of the school curriculum, including textbooks, individual teaching styles, and instructional techniques. The resource teacher will need to take the initiative in becoming aware of all facets of the curriculum to which learning disabled students will be exposed. Only in this way will he or she be prepared to help students and teachers alike enhance the total educational program for LD students.

Communicating with Teachers

Communication between the resource teacher and the regular classroom teacher is, in all probability, the one area that can lead to either success or failure of a mainstreaming approach for exceptional students. The following suggestions may aid in more successful and systematic communication between these two teachers.

Step 1.
Setting up conferences.

• Resource teacher-regular classroom teacher conferences should be scheduled at least once each month if there is to be a cooperative effort for the student's academic and social growth. These meetings should be scheduled at a convenient time for the classroom teacher and should last no longer than ten or fifteen minutes. If any special information or materials (such as student grades, test papers, etc.) will be needed, the teacher should be made aware of this several days before the conference.

Step 2.
Conducting the conference.

• The conference should be friendly and comfortable, but at the same time, businesslike. The less "small talk" that takes place in the beginning, the more productive the conference will be.

The resource teacher should begin the conference by reporting what the LD student is doing in the resource room and what progress is being made. He or she can then ask about the student's work in the regular classroom and the kinds of problems being encountered. At this point, specific plans can be made for both the regular classroom and the resource room.

While making suggestions for regular classroom activities, the resource teacher should always be prepared to assist in some way in the resource room. This may take the form of helping the student with vocabulary words, helping the teacher find or prepare materials, having the student read supplementary material in the resource room, or simply showing interest in the student's classroom work. The resource teacher should convey specific ways in which he or she will assist and *then* ask, "What else can I do to help?"

It is the responsibility of the resource teacher to keep a record of these meetings and what plans were made for each student. If plans are made for adjustments in the regular classroom, the resource teacher will need to check periodically with the teacher to see if the plan is working or if additional adjustments need to be made, etc. If the resource teacher plans to help the student on a particular skill or study for a test, etc., he or she will need to report the progress made to the teacher. In each child's folder, simple conference forms such as the following should be filed. It is also a good idea to give a copy to the regular classroom teacher.

With this information available, the resource

*Student*_____

*Date*_____

*Teacher*_____

*Discussed*_____

_____

_____

*Plans made*_____

_____

_____

_____

*Next conference scheduled*_____

teacher can immediately see what follow-ups need to be made and when additional conferences need to be held. Without this written reminder, many conferences may be wasted time, as both resource teacher and regular classroom teacher are busy with other things and forget just what plans were made.

Before a conference is completed, plans should be made for a follow-up conference. The date should be set, and both parties should be aware of what is expected of them in the interval.

Step 3.
Follow-up conference.

- The follow-up conference is a time to assess the progress made and reasons for the success or lack of success of the actions taken. The resource teacher will need to be adept at analyzing the reasons for failure as well as success, and will need to be always ready with praise and encouragement for the teacher's efforts.

The conference form from the previous meeting is a ready reference to begin the conference. The resource teacher may again report what has happened with the student in the resource room and then ask how the plans worked in the regular classroom. Together the two teachers will decide what changes need to be made and what additional things can be done. Conference forms are again completed and a date set for the next conference.

The resource teacher may also want to receive periodic written reports from the regular classroom teachers. An appropriate time to ask for these reports is at the end of each reporting period. The following forms may be used for this purpose:

REPORT FROM REGULAR CLASS TO LD RESOURCE ROOM

*Student*_____ *Subject*_____
*Grade this reporting period*_____
*Date*_____
Was this student able to read class material?
*Yes*_____ *No*_____
Did this student put forth effort in the classroom?
*Yes*_____ *No*_____
Did this student complete home assignments?
*Yes*_____ *No*_____
Are there any special problems with this student?
_____
_____

*Do we need a special conference? Yes*_____ *No*_____
*If yes, preferred date and time*_____

_____
Signature

Periodically, the resource teacher will need to see teachers in groups to discuss ongoing problems of learning disabled students in general and the problems being encountered by the students in their school specifically. The teachers as a group can discuss behaviors exhibited in different situations and also help generate suggestions for classroom adjustments suitable to individual needs.

A letter such as the following may announce such a meeting:

To: All Teachers
From: H.K. Boucher, Principal

On Wednesday, November 24, the LD Resource Teacher will hold a workshop for the regular classroom teachers. The workshop will be conducted all day, but each subject teacher will only attend during his/her planning period. We apologize for taking away your planning period for one day, but feel we have some practical suggestions for use with the learning disabled students in your class. We also need input from you as to appropriate classroom adjustments.

The coordination between the resource room and the regular classroom has been the major reason for the success of the LD program. We appreciate your cooperation thus far and look forward to seeing you Wednesday.

In addition to scheduled conferences and meetings and periodic written reports, the resource teacher should be as visible to regular classroom teachers as possible. He or she should "drop by" informally after school to say "How are things going?"

"How is Tommy doing?"

The resource room teacher must work extra hard and, often, extra hours to keep up with each student, his or her regular classroom progress, as well as resource room progress. By keeping teachers informed and "helping them to help the students," the success of the total program will be greatly enhanced.

Summary

Communication between the resource teacher and regular classroom teachers cannot be overemphasized. Formal and informal communication is essential for total program effectiveness. Conferences, written reports, and group meetings allow essential interactions and cooperative planning to take place, and a coordinated effort results, making the child's educational program more continuous and meaningful.

Communicating with Parents

Parents should be kept informed on a regular basis of ongoing progress and activities in the resource room. Parent-teacher conferences should be scheduled at least twice a year. Much better cooperation from the home is achieved if parents really "know" their child's teacher. Conferences to report student progress and to simply show parents that the teacher is indeed concerned about the child's progress are perhaps the best means of gaining the parents' understanding and cooperation. Friendliness, openness, and honesty are essentials for an effective parent conference.

Conferences should never be held for the sole purpose of reporting "bad" behavior or trouble at school. They should begin and end with a positive note. Examples of the student's work should be shown to the parent and an explanation of the resource room activities given. If there are special problems with the student or expected progress is not being seen, the parent's help may be solicited. Together, the teacher and parent can look at the problem and arrive at possible solutions.

In the course of the conference the parent may ask, "What can I do at home to help?" The resource teacher should always be prepared with suggestions and have materials available to give to the parent upon request.

If parents are unable or unwilling to come to the school for a conference, the resource teacher needs to find other means of communication. Often, teachers assume wrongly that parents are uninterested in their child's school progress, since "they never come for conferences" or respond negatively to attempts to get them to come to school when there is a problem with their child. If the truth were known, there are probably few parents who are truly uninterested in their child's school life. There are many parents who work during school hours and find it difficult to come to the school for conferences, and there are probably many parents who have had mostly negative interactions with school personnel, being called only when there is "trouble" and therefore look upon all requests to come for conferences as an attempt to report trouble. There are others who just simply do not feel comfortable with teachers, who have sometime in their lives been made to feel uncomfortable with teachers.

If parents are simply unable to come to the school because of work schedules, transportation, or other reasons, the resource teacher should try to find time to visit the home. A telephone call or note should precede the visit to arrange a convenient time and express the reasons for the meeting.

If parents are reluctant or unwilling to schedule a conference time, other steps can be taken. A telephone call occasionally to report "good" things can help to break the ice. A handwritten note accompanying a good paper is another means to open communication channels. After several of these, the parent will probably be less reluctant to come to the school for a conference or have the teacher visit the home.

Parent workshops are another excellent way to communicate with parents. The resource teacher and guidance counselor may work cooperatively to present these workshops. The following letter explains one type of workshop:

Dear Parents:

During the placement of your son into the learning disabilities Resource Room Program, I enjoyed meeting individually with many of you. One of the most frequently asked questions was, "How can I help my child at home?"

On Thursday, February 12, 1976, I will hold a "workshop for parents" in the South Junior High Library from 4:30 to 5:30 PM. At this meeting I hope that I can give you some practical ideas to use with your son at home. Also, a filmstrip that explains the nature of the learning disabled student will be shown.

Both the guidance counselor and I will be available for questions. I'm looking forward to meeting with you.

Sincerely yours,

Bruce Ambrose
LD Resource Teacher

A couple of days before the meeting, this reminder may be sent:

This is a reminder that on February 12, 1976, there will be a workshop for parents of students using the LD Resource Room.

At the workshop I hope to give you some practical ideas to help your son at home.

There will also be an interesting filmstrip and a question and answer time.

Hope to see you there.

Bruce Ambrose
LD Resource Teacher

Some helpful hints to give parents are:

1. Set up a scheduled time for your son or daughter to study (stick to it).
2. Have the home environment as structured and consistent as possible. Give this student chores to perform as a helping member of the family.
3. Be consistent in your discipline.
4. Be honest and understanding.
5. Praise the child.

The filmstrip *A Walk in Another Pair of Shoes* is excellent for use with parents.

The resource teacher may also initiate meetings to help organize local chapters of the Association for Children with Learning Disabilities. The state president or other state officer may be invited as a guest speaker.

Another program may feature resource room materials. The students could also attend this meeting which helps explain and demonstrate the use of materials. Examples of the student's work could also be available.

A spin off effect of parent workshops is that when parents of learning disabled students get together, they are able to share common experiences and begin to realize that others have had similar problems with their children. They will want to know how the problems were handled. They will feel less alone. Discussion should be encouraged for these reasons. Interest in further meetings will probably be heightened because of this common bond.

Periodic written progress reports should also be sent to parents. Often, every two weeks is not too frequent. A progress report such as the following may be used:

LD RESOURCE ROOM PROGRESS REPORT

Date_____

Student_____
Parent or Guardian_____
Resource Teacher_____

| | *Progress* (check *X*) | |
Basic Subjects	*Satisfactory*	*Unsatisfactory*
Arithmetic		
Reading		
Spelling		
Handwriting		
Behavior		

Attendance   1   2   3   4   5   6   7   8   9   10 days

Teacher's Remarks:
Parent's Remarks:
Conference Desired by Teacher_____
By Parent _____
Preferred Date and Time_____
Parent's Signature_____

COMPONENT 3.
COUNSELOR TRAINING SEQUENCE
A Message to Staff Development Leaders

For many LD adolescents, instructional adjustments alone
are not sufficient to insure their successful participation in the
mainstream. There is no guarantee that, even if provided for
educationally, LD students will accept help and will cooperate
with teachers and other students. Frustration resulting from
many years of failure in regular classes, segregation in special
classes, and abuse from thoughtless classmates and adults in the
school has often lowered the self-esteem and raised the defenses
of LD adolescents. They have defined themselves as losers, feel
a certain security in that role, and are suspicious of anyone who
suddenly seems to care about helping them become winners.

Although the severity of the damage to LD student self-
esteem varies greatly, depending upon each adolescent's past
experiences, most students need some help in adapting emotionally as well as intellectually to mainstreaming. Classroom
teachers, as previously suggested in Component 1, can conduct
classroom activities that help to strengthen self-acceptance and
acceptance of others in all students, LD students included.
However, classroom teachers are generally not professionally

equipped to systematically help LD adolescents with their social-emotional problems. Such help is better given by the school counselor in group and individual counseling sessions.

The purposes of the training procedures that follow are to help make school counselors aware of the emotional problems of LD students and to help them structure a counseling approach within which they can apply their professional expertise.

Training Procedures

OBJECTIVE: After completing this training sequence, school counselors will be able to organize and conduct an effective group counseling program with LD students.

Awareness Training

Training procedures for counselors assume that they are aware of and proficient in a number of general counseling techniques that are appropriate for LD adolescents. However, it cannot be assumed that they are aware of the characteristics and needs of LD students. The activities previously described for classroom teachers can be used to build counselor awareness of these behavioral characteristics and learning problems. In addition, the following supplementary activities are suggested to help counselors focus more specifically on the social-emotional needs of LD students:

1. Articles on learning disabilities written for school counselors are available in professional journals such as the *School Counselor*. Some recommended articles include:

- "The Secondary School Counselor and Learning Disabilities" (Humes, 1974).
- *The Child With Learning Disabilities and Guidance* (Anderson, 1970).

2. Contact with classroom and resource room teachers is particularly useful to counselors in identifying specific social-emotional problems of LD students in the school. Teachers can share their perceptions of the adjustment problems of their LD

students in several ways. One way is to submit social-emotional profiles of their LD students to the counselor. Profiles such as the one shown in Figure 6 can be submitted periodically and alert the counselor to problems for which group or individual counseling can be a solution. The counselor can assume that a problem actually exists and justifies counseling if he receives similar profiles from several of a student's teachers.

Another means to awareness of the social-emotional problems of LD students is through brief periodic meetings with the resource teacher and classroom teachers. These conferences can be held individually or with a group of teachers, need not last longer than ten to thirty minutes (depending on the number of people involved), and should be scheduled five or six times

LD STUDENT COUNSELING PROFILE

Student_____   To the teacher: Indicate the extent
Teacher_____   to which the behaviors
Counselor_____   listed below are
Date_____   problems for the LD
                                                    student.

Problem	No Problem	Slight Problem	Substantial Problem	Extremely Serious Problem	Things the Counselor Should Know
1. Shy, withdrawn, nonparticipating in group					
2. Aggressive, hostile, fights with peers					
3. Lacks self-confidence, low self-esteem					
4. Denies learning problems exist, refuses help					
5. Does not respond to encouragement					
6. Anxious, fearful, overworked					
7. Aggressive, rude toward teacher					
8. Other (list)					

Figure 6.

during the year, or as often as needed. Initial conferences allow teachers to elaborate on profile information, providing the counselor with a more in-depth awareness of the students' problems. Subsequent meetings can be used to share counseling approaches used with LD students and evaluate behavior changes resulting from counseling sessions.

Summary

Awareness training for school counselors should consist of understanding of the general characteristics of LD adolescents through the teacher awareness activities suggested in Component 1 (pp. 36-39); understanding of the social-emotional problems of LD adolescents through selected articles; and awareness of the specific social-emotional problems of students in their own school through student profiles and conferences with teachers.

Counseling with the LD Student

Effective counseling with LD adolescents can help these students to adapt socially and emotionally to the regular classroom, creating in them an openness to and acceptance of instructional assistance from their teachers and classmates. The following is a suggested three-step counseling procedure for use with LD students, within which the counselors can apply their own counseling approaches.

Step 1.
Setting up counseling sessions.

- A series of six to eight one-hour group counseling sessions is suggested as an adequate framework for exploring common feelings and problems and for planning ways of coping with those problems. Follow-up sessions can then be scheduled on an individual or group basis as needed, to assess present coping behaviors and to explore additional problems.

- A counseling group of no more than five members is recommended, with three to four members being ideal. Group sessions should be voluntary; no student should be pressured into participation. Counseling sessions should be held at a regularly scheduled time agreeable to the counselor, teachers, and students and should take place in a quiet setting away from any possible interruption.

Step 2.
Conducting counseling sessions.

- The specific approaches used to help LD adolescents explore common problems and learn coping behaviors is left to the professional discretion of the counselor. However, it is important that, whatever counseling approach is used, the sessions help students clearly identify social-emotional problems for which solutions are possible.

- The first two or three sessions can be devoted to exploring feelings and identifying problems. The next two or three meetings should help students learn effective behaviors for coping with problems. Students should be given the opportunity within the counseling group to try out coping behaviors in simulated problem situations. By role playing teachers and students, they can practice particular behaviors and learn to deal with different responses to those behaviors. Given their best efforts, LD students will not always receive cooperative and helping responses from teachers and other students. They must also learn to survive negative treatment and rejection of their coping behaviors. Students should be given the opportunity during the last several meetings to assess the effects of behaviors which they have actually tried out in their relationships with teachers and classmates. No students should complete the sessions without an arsenal of coping behaviors designed to help them succeed in the regular classroom. Situations such as the following may require students to use coping behaviors:

1. The teacher fails to adequately provide instructional adjustments for the LD student.
2. The teacher's expectations for the LD student are too high or low.
3. The teacher views the student as disruptive and uncooperative.
4. Other students make fun of the LD student's learning problem.

Counselors and LD students are encouraged to make definite commitments to coping strategies by documenting planned behaviors on a planning sheet such as the one shown in Figure 7. The counselor may have to help the student fill out the planning sheet.

Step 3. *Counseling session follow-up.*

• Following the completion of initial counseling sessions, the counselor's services to the LD student should continue as needed throughout the school year. It is expected that the counselor will have established a trusting and helping relationship with each LD student during the sessions. This relationship should encourage students to meet either individually or as a group with him to assess their progress in coping in the mainstream and to pursue addi-

PLANNING SHEET FOR COPING BEHAVIORS

Student _____

Counselor _____

Date	Interacting With	Problem	LD student Coping Behavior	Expected Outcome	Actual Outcome
2/2/77	Teacher	• Teacher shows frustration with my slowness completing assignment.	• Thank teacher for trying to be patient with me. • Assure teacher I am trying my best to complete assignment. • Give teacher specific time when I think I can be through with assignment.	• Teacher will cooperate and extend time for completion of assignment.	• Teacher did extend time for completing assignment. • Assignment completed within agreed upon time.

Figure 7.

tional problems as they arise. The number and frequency of follow-up sessions depends on need and is left to the judgment of the counselor and students.

- During and following the initial group sessions, the counselor should maintain close communication with classroom teachers, continually soliciting their perceptions of interactions with LD students and observations of interactions among LD students and their classmates. As the group counseling sessions progress, the counselor should communicate to the teachers ways in which they can make the social-emotional environment more secure for the LD student. At the same time, it is

STUDENT COPING PROFILE FOR TEACHERS

Student_____*Sam*_____

Teacher_____*Mrs. Jones*_____

Counselor_____*Mrs. Smith*_____

Date	Adjustment Problem	Student Coping Plan	Suggested Teacher Support	Teacher Observation of Student Progress
2/22/77	Sam anxious about not meeting teacher expectation in completing class assignments within set time period.	• Verbally assure teacher of intention to complete assignments as quickly as possible. • Give teacher specific time when he thinks he can reasonably finish. • Ask teacher's acceptance of this time.	• Give student verbal encouragement and praise in completing assignments. • Accept fact that student's disability causes him to work slower and more deliberately. • Help student to realistically set time limits on his class work.	2/29/77 • Conflicts with student related to assignment completion somewhat reduced. • Student seems less anxious in class.

Figure 8.

important that the counselor not violate the confidentiality of counseling sessions by revealing personal confidences shared by LD students during the session. The counselor must simply use good judgment in this area.

- As previously described, one means of communicating with classroom teachers about LD students is through conferences. In addition to conferences, another way that counselors can communicate with teachers about the social-emotional problems of LD students is with a short communication form, such as the one presented in Figure 8. The form can be used by the counselor to help teachers become aware of problems of LD students and the behaviors which the student plans to use for coping in the regular classroom. This awareness should encourage teachers to support student coping efforts.

Summary

Effective counseling with LD adolescents consists of three basic procedures designed to help them adapt socially and emotionally to the regular classroom:

1. Considerations in setting up the counseling sessions.
2. Conducting counseling sessions that help students identify problems and plan appropriate coping behaviors.
3. Following up counseling sessions with both LD students and teachers to assess the effects of coping behaviors in the regular classroom.

Monitoring Counseling Activities

As counselors begin working with LD students, they need to periodically evaluate their application of the three counseling procedures. Form F is provided as a self-assessment sheet designed to help counselors reflect on the quality of their performance of the counseling tasks. Although the assessment sheet is somewhat subjective in nature, it can provide a general guide to critical analysis of the counselor's work with the LD students.

It is recommended that the counselor solicit help from other counselors or the staff development leader within the school to review counseling activities. Third-party observations and judgments can often reveal needs for improvement that are overlooked in self-evaluation.

Form F

ASSESSMENT OF PERFORMANCE OF COUNSELING TASKS

Counselor _____

Reviewer _____ Date _____

Counseling Tasks	Performance Acceptable	Comments and Suggestions for Improvement
1. Preliminary identification of LD student social-emotional problems from teacher conferences.		
2. Conditions, i.e. time, place, number of participants, and number of sessions, conducive to productive counseling.		
3. Assists students in identifying specific problems; tentative solutions (coping behaviors) proposed and practiced within the counseling group.		
4. Assists students in completing coping behavior planning sheets; behaviors relate to problem; behaviors reasonable, should lead to expected outcome.		
5. Follow-up counseling sessions held; outcomes of coping behaviors assessed; additional problems discussed.		
6. Follow-up communication with teachers established; student coping profiles used.		

COMPONENT 4.
INSTRUCTIONAL LEADERSHIP TRAINING SEQUENCE
A Message to Staff Development Leaders

Success of any staff development program within a school depends greatly on the quality of leadership exerted in the implementation of the program. The importance of effective leadership in conducting the *training sequence for classroom teaching* cannot be overemphasized. Without a knowledgeable and committed leader, staff development activities for classroom mainstreaming simply will not succeed.

A potential staff development leader does not have to be an "expert" in the area of learning disabilities. However, the leader should possess a broad knowledge of basic principles of instruction, be able to relate positively to classroom teachers, and be in a position to at least influence administrative and organizational decisions within the school. The resource teacher is a logical candidate for this position, providing he or she has the requisite instructional skills and can relate to classroom teachers. If not, an alternative choice might be the school's curriculum coordinator, a master teacher, or the principal. Still, the resource teacher must play a primary role in staff development, providing the staff development leader with technical assistance about learning disabilities and meeting frequently with classroom teachers to share information about LD students. A school may wish to assign leadership to a staff development team composed of two or more leadership personnel.

Although instructional expertise is most important, the staff development leader(s), if not the principal, must have strong administrative support from the principal. Mainstreaming the LD students may necessitate administrative action related to such requirements as cumbersome schedule changes and released time for teachers and students. Lack of strong principal commitment to making these administrative adjustments will likely subvert the best of instructional attempts to assist teachers in adjusting their teaching for LD students.

The activities and procedures previously described under *training sequence for classroom teaching* are intended to be administered by the in-school staff development leader and should provide adequate guidance as written. Outside consultant assistance is not required. Specific training for staff development leaders focuses primarily on awareness of the characteristics and problems of LD students, on a monitoring procedure for helping teachers plan, and on a technique for providing them with feedback on the quality of their instruction with LD students. The monitoring procedure consists specifically of a *planning review conference, classroom observation, and a follow-up conference.* If a number of schools in the school district are using this staff development approach to mainstreaming, district office leadership personnel or a consultant can conduct leadership training with staff development leaders from a number of schools. However, where only a few schools are involved, this training procedure can be self-administered by the staff development leader.

Training Procedures

OBJECTIVE: After completing this training sequence, staff development leaders will be able to effectively monitor teacher training activities through structured planning conferences, classroom observation, and follow-up evaluation conferences.

Awareness Training

This approach to instructional leadership training assumes that participants already possess general knowledge of the principles of instruction and can communicate effectively with teachers. However, staff development leaders may not be aware of the characteristics and learning problems of LD adolescents. The awareness activities for classroom teachers previously described (pp. 36-39) are also appropriate for the instructional leaders. The leader, responsible for conducting awareness activities with teachers, needs to assume the role of both learner and leader, thoroughly reviewing suggested materials prior to use with teachers and then acting as leader and participant in the activities with the staff members.

The Planning Review Conference

As teachers begin to plan instructional adjustments for their LD students and later, when they begin to incorporate adjustments into more individualized instructional approaches, they need to receive as much feedback as possible on how well they are doing. Planning errors, if undetected, can lead to failure of implementation and ultimately to discouraged and disillusioned teachers who abandon their efforts to help LD students. The staff development leader, by monitoring teacher planning, can insure that they develop plans with high potential for success. The following is a three-step procedure recommended to staff development leaders for conducting a planning review conference:

Step 1.
*Scheduling
conference
time and
place.*

• Conferences are best scheduled several days ahead of time with individual teachers, preferably during their daily planning time. The staff development leader should go to the teacher's classroom when possible to permit easy access to materials which may be used with the LD student. A specific time limit should be set for the conference. Ten to fifteen minutes is most often sufficient. Frequent short conferences are preferable to infrequent long ones. If elaborate unit or activity package plans are being reviewed, they should be submitted to the leader and read beforehand to permit efficient use of time during the conference.

Step 2.
Conducting the conference.

• During the conference time, the leader's task is to help the teacher determine the appropriateness of planned adjustments for increasing the LD student's chances for success in class activities. This can be best accomplished through a series of clarifying questions that encourage the teacher to be analytical about his or her plans. The questions parallel the planning steps on Forms A and B presented in the *classroom teaching* component (pages 42 & 44). Clarifying questions can lead to more specificity on the planning forms where needed. The following are examples of clarifying questions which the staff development leader can ask the teacher:

Planning — Ask the teacher such questions as:

A. • What are the objectives of your lesson?
  • What is it you will be doing with your class?
  • What activities will your students be involved in?
  • How long will activities last?
  • What performances will your students be expected to demonstrate?
  • What materials will your students be using?

B. • What problems will your LD student have in achieving lesson objectives?
  • What difficulties do you anticipate your LD student will have in participating in class activities?
  • What trouble will your LD student have in using lesson materials?

- What problems will your LD student have in demonstrating his knowledge or his ability to perform a skill or activity?
- What past evidence do you have that he will have the problems you describe?

C. • What adjustments are you going to make to help your LD student overcome or compensate for problems he will have in participating in class activities?
- What will you do to insure that your LD student can successfully meet your lesson objective?
- How can you eliminate the barriers to successful performance for your LD student?
- How are you going to make sure he achieves successfully?
- How are your adjustments related to his learning problems you have identified?

- As inconsistencies between proposed adjustments, student learning problems, and intended learning outcomes become apparent during the conference, the staff development leader can assist the teacher in revision of plans at that time.

Step 3. Completing the conference.

- The planning conference should be completed within the agreed-upon time even if more discussion seems to be needed. This forces the leader and teacher to adhere strictly to the task and will eventually result in a better use of time. As previously stated, ten- to fifteen-minute conferences are recommended.
- The staff development leader may find that some teachers need considerable assistance in planning for instruction with LD students, assistance which cannot be adequately given in a ten-minute conference. However, this assistance can often be given more effectively in a series of

short conferences over an extended period of time than in one or two long sessions which may overwhelm and discourage the teacher. Also, actual implementation of plans often reveals problems and weaknesses more emphatically to teachers than any advice from a staff development leader. Teachers, like students, learn from experience.

- Although it is not necessary for the staff development leader to observe the implementation of all teaching plans, frequent observations should be scheduled as a means of providing constructive feedback to teachers. When a leader intends to observe, he or she should schedule the observation with the teacher at the end of the planning conference. The teacher and leader should agree on the place, time, and purpose of the observation.

The Classroom Observation

The effectiveness of any instructional adjustments planned for an LD student can only be determined as the adjustments are actually made in the classroom. Appropriate planning can be totally negated by inappropriate implementation. Therefore, teachers are encouraged in the teacher training component (p. 34) to carefully assess their instruction. However, teachers are sometimes too involved in the teaching process to objectively evaluate their instructional strengths and weaknesses. Classroom observations by the staff development leader can be a reasonable objective means to providing teachers with feedback regarding the quality of their instruction with LD students. The following three-step observation procedure, recommended to staff development leaders, is not intended to be a highly systematic interaction analysis process, but rather a simple structure to facilitate professional dialogue between leaders and teachers.

Step 1.   • The staff development leader should prepare

Preparing to observe. for the observation by making certain he or she is aware of the planned adjustments being implemented (having a photocopy of the teacher's planning sheet would be helpful); making certain he or she knows which LD student(s) are receiving adjustments; and coming to the class at the time agreed on in the planning session. The leader need *not* try to make notes during the observation. Note taking often arouses student and teacher suspicion and can distract the leader's full attention from what the LD student is doing.

Step 2. *Observing the LD student.*

- During the observation, the leader's task is to determine the extent to which the implementation of planned adjustments is contributing to the LD student's success.

- A list of questions on observation Form G is provided to guide the observer in judging the quality of the instruction in promoting LD student success. The leader should observe the student(s) in terms of the questions, but should not try to complete the form until after the observation. If possible, during the observation, the leader should talk with the LD student and other students about what they are doing.

Step 3. *Completing the observation.*

- Classroom observation, like the planning review conference, can be more productive if times are short and frequent. This is particularly true if there are a large number of teachers to observe. Fifteen-minute observations should be sufficient to gain information for later discussion with teachers. All questions on the observation form will not necessarily be pertinent to any one observation. The leader may decide to focus on only one aspect of instruction during the observations; the leader should be able to get reasonably accurate pictures of how LD students and their teachers are doing.

- When the observation is complete, the leader should arrange a follow-up conference time with the teacher before leaving the room, if possible. The leader should then make notations as appropriate on the observation form.

Form G

MONITORING GUIDELINE
OBSERVATION FORM

II. *Implementation - Class Observation* —Observe the LD student in the class and answer the following questions:

A. What evidence is there that the teacher is making adjustments for the LD student as planned?

B. What evidence is there that the teacher actions are either enhancing or subverting the intentions of the adjustments?

C. What evidence exists that the LD student was being treated as an integral part of the class?

D. How would you rate the interaction between teacher and LD student?

Negative		No Interaction		Positive
1	2	3	4	5

E. How do you rate the LD student's attitude?

Negative		Neutral		Positive
1	2	3	4	5

F. What teacher actions are needed for better implementation of the planned adjustments?

G. What additional adjustments by the teacher seem to be needed for the LD student?

Post-Observation Conference

Teachers rarely receive constructive feedback from another professional on the quality of their classroom instruction. Yet, they are constantly expected to implement new approaches and try out new behaviors with little indication as to whether or not they are "doing it right." The purpose of the post-observation conference is to help teachers improve their instructional skills by providing them feedback on how well they are working with LD students. As with the planning review conference, a three-step procedure is recommended to staff development leaders for conducting the post-observation conference.

Step 1.   • The post-observation conferences should be

Scheduling conference time and place. held as soon after the observation as possible, preferably on the same day, when both teacher and observer perceptions are fresh. Like the planning conference and the observation periods, post-conference time should be from ten to fifteen minutes in length.

Step 2. Conducting the conference.

• The post-conference is not intended as time for the staff development leader to tell teachers what they did wrong. Rather, it is an opportunity to share perceptions of strengths and weaknesses about instruction of LD students. The leader can help teachers gain insight into their teaching of LD students through a series of clarifying questions. The questions parallel the evaluation questions presented on Form C.

Follow-up

A. Ask teacher such questions as —

  • How did your LD student do with the lesson?

  • To what extent did your adjustments help your LD student successfully complete the activity or lesson?

  • What difference did you see in your LD student's class behavior?

  • How did you determine the extent of your LD student's success with the activity or lesson?

  • How do you account for your LD student's success or failure?

  • What objective evidence do you have? What subjective evidence do you have?

  • How will you change your instruction with the LD student in the future?

  • What additional adjustments do you think are needed for your LD student?

B. Share your observations with the teacher.

C. Help the teacher plan additional adjustments.

- The questions should encourage teachers to express their perceptions of their work with LD students. During the discussion, the leader can confirm and reinforce teachers' perceptions with his or her own observations. The leader may also need at times to challenge teachers' perceptions when they are inconsistent with observations. However, this must be done with tact and in a helping way to avoid teacher defensiveness or feelings of failure. Feedback to teachers should emphasize teaching strengths as well as weaknesses.

Step 3.
Completing
the
conference.

- Post-observation conferences need not extend beyond the time limit set if the staff development leader limits discussion and feedback to only a few aspects of the observation. Leaders should resist the temptation to give teachers more feedback than they can accept and assimilate. Assistance in other areas of concern can be given in subsequent conferences.
- Conferences should end with the leader and teacher agreeing on some follow-up action to be taken by the teacher. This action can be written down on the teacher's evaluation form (Form C) and the leader's observation form (Form G). Examples of follow-up activities are:
  - Modification of adjustments that were tried and failed
  - Addition of new adjustments
  - Inclusion of adjustments in new instructional techniques

Training Activities

Staff development leaders, through their monitoring activities, can do much to enhance the quality of teacher planning and instruction. However, leaders themselves need help in monitoring their own activities. They need ways to assess their own leadership strengths and weaknesses and their effectiveness in helping teachers plan and implement high-quality instruction for LD students.

If several schools within a district are implementing this staff development approach, monitoring of staff development leaders can begin with an in-service session for leaders on conducting effective planning and post-observation conferences. The in-service training should be conducted by a district level curriculum leader. The following activities are among those which can be included in this in-service session:

- Activities for general awareness of the characteristics and learning problems of LD students (*see* section on *classroom teacher training*, p. 36).
- Planning for administrative support needed to sustain the mainstreaming approach.
- Orientation to monitoring conferences and organization procedures.
- Simulated conferences to give leaders practice in conducting planning and evaluation sessions with teachers. Simulated conferences can involve participants in role-playing dialogue between teacher and staff development leader. One participant can plan a series of adjustments for the student profiled on page 38, or the in-service leader can provide a profile and planned adjustments.

Two participants can role play the conference, using the format previously described. Other participants can serve as observers, giving feedback to the role players on the effectiveness of the staff development leader. Form H can be used as an observation sheet for analyzing the quality of the conference. The student profile on page 38 and a list of adjustments can also be used to simulate a post-observation conference. Participants can make up the events of the implementation-observation to serve as the basis for conference dialogue. Form H can again be used to guide analysis of the conference.

Following initial in-service training, Form H can be used as a general monitoring instrument to help staff development leaders assess their effectiveness in actual conference situations. Conferences can be taped and analyzed so another instructional leader within the school can observe and give feedback. Staff development leaders should frequently solicit feedback from teachers, as well as from colleague observers, as a means of developing and upgrading their monitoring proficiency.

Form H

MONITORING THE STAFF DEVELOPMENT LEADER

Staff Development Leader_____

Reviewer_____ Date_____

Conference Variables	Acceptable	Comments and Suggestions for Improvement
1. Conference conditions, i.e. time, place, conducive to productive planning.		
2. Length of conference appropriate, adhered to.		
3. Leader supportive, puts teacher at ease.		
4. Leader-teacher communication open, positive, shared.		
5. Leader uses clarifying questions to help teachers detect inconsistencies between planned adjustments and LD students' needs (planning conference).		
6. Leader assists teacher in revising planned adjustments as needed (planning conference).		
7. Leader uses clarifying questions to help teacher assess implementation of planned adjustments for LD students (post-observation conference).		
8. Leader assists teacher in projecting follow-up activities for LD students (post-observation conference).		

Summary

Staff development leaders need to assess on a continuous basis their own effectiveness in monitoring teacher instruction with LD students. Training for staff development leaders can focus on effective implementation of three monitoring procedures: the *planning review conference,* the *classroom observation,* and the *post-observation conference.*

PART IV

EVALUATION

SYSTEMATIC evaluation must be an integral component of any educational program, for in no other way will the persons involved know how well the program is working and how nearly the goals have been met. Evaluation should be ongoing and should provide feedback on every major facet of the program.

The process as well as product evaluation should be conducted. Evaluation should be used not only to determine if academic gains have been made, but used analytically to determine strengths and weaknesses of the program processes and what changes need to be made to make the program more effective. If student gains in academic or social areas are not as significant as had been hoped or if parents or teachers are not satisfied with the program or the children's progress, further investigation should lead to program changes and improvements. If this does not happen, the evaluation has been a waste of time and effort.

In a mainstreaming program such as the one described in this book, evaluation may be conducted in the following areas:

1. Student academic progress
2. Student self-concept growth and attitude change
3. Parental involvement and satisfaction with the program
4. Effectiveness of staff training activities and teacher satisfaction with the program

STUDENT ACADEMIC PROGRESS

Student academic progress can be measured in terms of whether or not the instructional objectives of the individualized educational program have been met. The resource teacher assesses skills on an ongoing basis and keeps daily records of the skills acquired. Locally developed tests can be used in the regular classrooms to determine student progress. These tests may be adapted for the LD student in the ways recommended in Suggested Instructional Adjustments for Students (*see* Appendix B).

In addition, a school or district may wish to use norm-referenced tests to determine the effectiveness of their program in relation to others or to determine if academic gains are significantly greater than they have been in the past. This is useful information for program evaluation; however, norm-referenced testing should never be the sole form of assessment, as it contributes little to the instructional programming for the child.

If norm-referenced tests are to be used for program evaluation, several tests that may serve the purpose are:

- *Metropolitan Achievement Test* (Durost et al., 1971).
- *California Achievement Test* (Tiegs and Clark 1970).
- *Stanford Achievement Test* (Madden et al., 1975).
- *Peabody Individual Achievement Test* (Dunn and Markwardt, 1970).

SELF-CONCEPT AND ATTITUDE CHANGE

Again, self-concept growth may be measured by norm-referenced tests designed for this purpose. Two such tests that seem appropriate for this age-group are the:

1. *Piers-Harris Self-Concept Scale* (Piers and Harris, 1969).
2. *Self-Observation Scale,* intermediate and/or junior level (Stenner and Katzenmeyer, 1975).

Student attitudes may be assessed with a student self-report questionnaire such as the one shown in Sample D. This questionnaire is designed to detect changes in attitudes toward school, self-concept, and other related personality factors, in addition to interpersonal relationships with parents, peers, and school personnel. The questions on this questionnaire, as well as the above norm-referenced tests, should be read to all students.

Sample D
STUDENT QUESTIONNAIRE

I would like to know if things are different for you at school this year. I will read you a statement. Think about the sentence and then check one of the blanks on your paper. *(Much more, more, the same, less,* or *much less.)*

1. I get along better with the other students.
2. My teachers are patient with me when I have problems with my work.
3. I like school this year.
4. My schoolwork seems easier.
5. My principal knows me better this year.
6. Other people understand my learning problems in school.
7. My guidance counselor has helped me understand my learning problems.
8. I have really improved my schoolwork in the resource room.
9. My mother helps me more with my homework.
10. My father helps me more with my homework.
11. My parents are more patient with me with my schoolwork.
12. My parents see my teacher more this year.
13. My parents are pleased with my homework.
14. The resource room has helped me do my schoolwork better in all my classes.
15. I feel better about myself.
16. Learning is more fun.
17. I know that I will continue to improve my schoolwork even though some subjects will be slow.
18. I have talked more with my principal this year.
19. If other children tease me about school, I can control myself because I understand myself better.
20. I know why it is important to do well in school.
21. I take pride in my accomplishments.
22. I feel that I'll be successful someday.
23. I think my teachers understand me better.

STAFF TRAINING

Teachers, counselors, and principals should be asked to complete questionnaires several times during the school year to assess the effectiveness of training activities. The evaluation questionnaire shown in Sample E may be used after three or four months of training. The results of this questionnaire will allow the staff development leader(s) to make process changes to correct problem areas reported by the respondents. A

Sample E

INTERIM EVALUATION QUESTIONNAIRE

Please Check One:

LD Resource Teacher_____

Counselor_____

Principal_____

Content Teacher_____, Subject Taught_____

Please circle the appropriate number and add comments where needed.

1. My knowledge of LD characteristics has increased as a result of in-service training.

1	2	3	4	5
Not at All		Somewhat		Greatly

Comments:

2. My understanding of the specific disabilities of the LD students I teach (counsel, observe) has increased.

1	2	3	4	5
Not at All		Somewhat		Greatly

Comments:

3. I have seen improvements in the academic performance of LD students as a result of new instructional methods used in the classroom.

1	2	3	4	5
Not at All		Somewhat		Greatly

Comments:

4. I have seen improvements in the academic performance of LD students as a result of resource room intervention.

1	2	3	4	5
Not at All		Somewhat		Greatly

Comments:

5. I have seen improvements in the behavior of LD students because of new instructional methods and/or resource room intervention.

1	2	3	4	5
Not at All		Somewhat		Greatly

Comments:

6. The techniques suggested by the staff development leader(s) seem appropriate for the LD students I teach and/or observe.

1	2	3	4	5
Not at All		Somewhat		Greatly

Comments:

Sample E *(continued)*
INTERIM EVALUATION QUESTIONNAIRE

7. To what extent is it possible to individualize in order to provide instruction for LD students in the regular classroom?

1	2	3	4	5
Little		Some		Great

Comments:

8. To what extent have the in-service meetings helped provide what is needed to work with LD students?

1	2	3	4	5
Little		Some		Great

Comments:

9. To what extent is the monitoring done by principals and counselors effective and helpful?

1	2	3	4	5
Little		Some		Great

Comments:

10. To what extent have classroom visitations by staff development leader(s) been helpful?

1	2	3	4	5
Little		Some		Great

Comments:

11. To what extent is resource room teacher and content area teacher communication frequent and effective?

1	2	3	4	5
Little		Some		Great

Comments:

12. To what extent is counselor and teacher communication concerning LD students frequent and effective?

1	2	3	4	5
Little		Some		Great

Comments:

13. To what extent is principal and teacher communication concerning LD students frequent and effective?

1	2	3	4	5
LIttle		Some		Great

Comments-

Please check those instructional techniques which you have used (or would like to use) and consider particularly promising for LD students.

Techniques I Have Used or Seen and Feel Are Promising for LD Students	Techniques I Would Like to Use or See Used	
_____	_____	Peer teaching, tutoring
_____	_____	Self-pacing
_____	_____	Small group learning
_____	_____	Manipulatives
_____	_____	Learning activity packages
_____	_____	Learning contracts
_____	_____	Learning centers
_____	_____	Formal drill
_____	_____	Tape recorder
_____	_____	Oral testing
_____	_____	Adjusting content amount
_____	_____	Time adjustments
_____	_____	Class discussion

The greatest need that I see right now is:

_____

_____

_____

_____

_____

_____

_____

_____

_____

year-end questionnaire, shown in Sample F, can be used when plans are being made for the next year.

PARENTAL INVOLVEMENT AND SATISFACTION

In order to evaluate changes in the areas of parental involvement and satisfaction, a parent questionnaire such as shown in Sample G can be completed by parents of LD students. Questionnaires can be mailed to parents with the cover letter shown.

Sample F

LD PROGRAM EVALUATION

1. Rank the degree to which you have seen improvement in the academic skills of LD students.

    _____Very much _____Much _____Some _____Little _____None
    Comments:

2. To what degree have you seen improvement in the behavior of LD students?

    _____Very much _____Much _____Some _____Little _____None
    Comments:

3. To what degree have you been successful in making instructional adjustments for the LD student?

    _____Very successful _____Successful _____Somewhat successful
    _____Not very successful _____Not at all successful
    Comments:

4. To what degree has your knowledge of LD characteristics increased as a result of program activities?

    _____Very much _____Much _____Some _____Little _____None
    Comments:

5. To what degree were the techniques suggested by program personnel appropriate for the LD students you teach?

    _____Very appropriate _____Appropriate _____Somewhat appropriate
    _____Not very appropriate _____Not at all appropriate
    Comments:

6. To what extent have the in-service meetings helped provide what is needed to work with LD students?

    _____Very much _____Much _____Some _____Little _____None
    Comments:

7. To what extent do you feel new instructional techniques used have helped *all* your students?

    _____Very much _____Much _____Some _____Little _____None
    Comments:

8. How would you rank the overall service of the resource room to your school?

    _____Excellent _____Above average _____Average _____Fair _____Poor
    Comments:

9. To what degree do you think the overall program has been successful in your school?

    _____Very successful _____Successful _____Somewhat successful
    _____Not very successful _____Not at all successful
    Comments:

10. What changes would you suggest in program activities for another year?

Sample G

Dear Parent:

Your child has participated in an educational program for children with learning problems during the past school year.

We are very interested in knowing how satisfied you were with this program. Please fill out the enclosed questionnaire and have your child return it to Mrs. Howard.

Thank you.

Sincerely,

A. E. Warfield
Principal
Eastside Middle School

Summary

Student academic achievement, self-concept and attitude change, and parental and teacher satisfaction are areas to be included in a program evaluation. Evaluation should be used to generate any needed changes and improvements in the program, as well as to indicate the effectiveness of the program.

Sample H
PARENT QUESTIONNAIRE

1. How satisfied were you with your child's progress in his school work?

    ____Very satisfied

    ____Satisfied

    ____Neither satisfied nor dissatisfied

    ____Very dissatisfied

2. Did your child's behavior improve in school this year?

    ____Very much

    ____It improved a little

    ____Stayed the same

    ____It was a little worse

    ____It was much worse

3. How many times did you see your child's resource room teacher this year?

    ____Once

    ____Twice

    ____Three times

    ____Other (please specify)

4. How many times did you see your child's guidance counselor this year?

    ____Once

    ____Twice

    ____Three times

    ____Other (please specify)

5. Do you better understand why your child has problems learning some school materials?

    ____Yes, I understand much better.

    ____Yes, I understand better.

    ____I understand things about the same.

    ____No, things are harder to understand.

    ____I don't understand at all.

6. Does your child seem to be happier in school this year?

    ____Yes, much happier.

    ____A little happier.

    ____He or she is about as happy as last year.

    ____He or she is not as happy this year.

    ____My child is very unhappy this year.

PART V

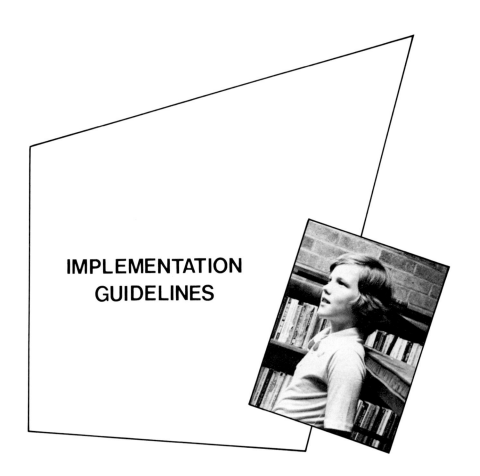

IMPLEMENTATION
GUIDELINES

ACTUAL implementation of a program of mainstreaming requires careful planning. This planning can involve the entire school staff or a smaller representative group who can submit the plan for total staff approval. In either case, the school staff must first be clear about what they intend to accomplish by mainstreaming. They must then make a commitment to a set of procedures, such as those described in Parts I through IV, for achieving their desired outcomes. Finally, they must assign responsibility and establish time limits for completion of tasks implicit in the procedures.

This section contains guidelines that the staff development leader can use to help structure the staff's steps toward full implementation of a mainstreaming program. The guidelines provide for selection, adaptation, and coordination of the procedures previously described in the sections on student identification, resource room preparation, staff training, and evaluation. If the implementation planning process includes teacher training, the guidelines in this section might best be used by a small planning committee already familiar with the procedures outlined in Parts I through IV. The guidelines should help a planning group provide for implementation of a well-coordinated mainstreaming program with a high potential for success.

The implementation guidelines which follow are presented as a five-step process:

1. Establishing a statement of general direction.
2. Developing a number of implementation objectives.
3. Specifying implementation activities for each objective.
4. Constructing a management document for sequencing activities, assigning responsibility, specifying resources and support needed, and establishing dates for completion of activities.
5. Evaluating the quality of the implementation plan.

Step 1. *Statement of direction.*
• The staff should first decide, in broadly defined terms, how they want to approach mainstreaming, what in general they want to accomplish. Do they want to mainstream all

children or only those less severely handicapped? Will mainstreaming affect the entire staff or only a select group of teachers? To what degree should the regular teaching staff provide for the needs of the LD student? What level of staff training will be provided? How often will students be mainstreamed? Consideration of questions like these can provide direction for development of specific implementation, objectives and activities.

- Sample statements of direction are presented on Form I, a form that can be used by the staff to facilitate planning for implementation.

Step 2. *Developing implementation objectives.*
- Once the general direction of the mainstreaming program is clearly stated, more specific implementation objectives can be developed. Using the statement(s) of direction agreed on in Step 1, the school staff can more specifically define what it is that they intend to achieve as a result of their mainstreaming efforts. Objectives should describe in detail expected outcomes in such areas as identification and scheduling of LD students, training of school staff, lines of communication among staff, and extent of services of LD students and evaluation.

- Sample implementation objectives, derived from the sample statements of direction (Step 1) are presented on Form I.

Step 3. *Implementation activities*
- Implementation objectives (Step 2) will be of little use to school staff unless they can translate them into concrete activities-tasks. The implementation activities, designed to achieve objectives, are the heart of the implementation process, for they represent the day-to-day actions of students and staff in accomplishment of their intentions related to mainstreaming.

- In developing implementation activities-tasks,

staff should, as systematically as possible, generate activities for each objective stated in Step 2. The number of activities-tasks for any objective will vary with the nature of the objective. Some objectives may be attained through one activity, while others require a series of tasks.

- Sample implementation activities, derived from sample objectives, are presented on Form I.

Step 4.
Management document

- Implementation activities-tasks are more readily accomplished when responsibility for their completion is firmly fixed and when time limits are imposed. When activities, persons responsible for them, and their completion dates are sequenced in logical order, there tends to be less ambiguity about what is to be done, who is to do it, and when it is to be completed. What results is a management document that can be used to guide implementation of the mainstreaming program.
- Form J is a partial sample of a management document.

Step 5.
Evaluating implementation plans

- Once Steps 1 through 4 of the implementation process have been completed, the staff should evaluate the quality of their plans prior to actual implementation. When this is done and necessary revisions in plans are made, the mainstreaming process should proceed more smoothly and efficiently.
- Objectives, activities and the management plan can be assessed by the staff development leader, a small staff planning committee, or the entire school faculty.
- Individuals evaluating the implementation plans should use a common set of criteria to achieve reasonable consistency in the evaluation process. A suggested list of criteria is provided on Form K. The list is not exhaustive. Staff may want to add or delete certain criteria to meet their own local needs.

Form I
IMPLEMENTATION PLANNING SHEET

I. Statements of General Direction

    A. To mainstream (into all curriculum areas) all LD students presently being served in the resource room.

    B. To help all faculty members to be aware of the needs of LD students; to prepare a select group of staff members to teach LD students in the regular classroom.

    C. To provide administrative, instructional, and counseling support services to these teachers.

II. Implementation Objectives

    A. By October the entire school faculty will be aware of the characteristics and needs of LD students; at least one-fourth of the faculty will have volunteered to begin training to teach LD students in the regular classroom setting.

    B. By November an efficient system of communication between classroom teachers, counselors, and resource teachers will have been established.

    C. By December approximately____LD students from the resource room will be mainstreamed in the classes of teachers who have been prepared to teach them.

    D. By May approximately____LD students will have participated in ____ group counseling sessions designed to prepare and support them as they return to the regular classroom.

III. Implementation Activities

    Objective: By September the entire school faculty will be aware of the characteristics and needs of LD students; at least one-fourth of the faculty will have volunteered to begin training to teach LD students in the regular classroom.

    Activities:

1. Two-day in-service session of awareness activities prior to opening of school for total faculty.

2. One day of follow-up awareness in-service training at midyear for total faculty.

3. Initial two-day training session for regular classroom teachers volunteering to work with mainstreamed LD students during the year.

4. Teachers follow five-step procedure in planning, implementing, and evaluating the effect of instructional adjustments on LD student achievement.

5. Monthly follow-up teacher sharing sessions regarding success and failure of instructional adjustments (approximately forty-five minutes per session).

IMPLEMENTATION PLANNING SHEET

Objective: By November an efficient system of communication between classroom teachers, counselors,
and resource teacher will have been established.

  Activities:

1. Resource teacher will develop a communication form to
   provide for continuous exchange of information with
   classroom teachers about LD student strengths, weaknesses, problems, successes, and recommendations.
2. Resource teacher will be released one full day per month
   to help teachers assess their work with LD students and
   plan instructional adjustments.
3. School counselor will develop a communication form to
   provide for continuous exchange of information with
   classroom teachers about the social-emotional status of
   LD students and the strategies used to ease their adaptation to the regular classroom.
4. Counselors will meet with classroom teachers at least
   once every six weeks.

Objective: By December approximately_____LD students
from the resource room will be mainstreamed
in the classes of teachers who have been prepared to teach them.

  Activities:

1. Students will be scheduled into regular classrooms in as
   many subject areas as possible.
2. Each mainstreamed student will be scheduled into the
   resource room for a minimum of one period per day.
3. Students' grades and standarized test scores analyzed as
   an indication of achievement success under mainstreaming.

Objective: By May approximately___LD students will have
participated in___group counseling sessions designed to prepare and support them as they return to the regular classroom.

  Activities:

1. Each LD student mainstreamed will participate in six
   one-hour group counseling sessions for six consecutive
   weeks followed by a minimum of one individual session with the counselor each month throughout the re-
   mainder of the year.
2. The counselor will help each student develop a set of
   behaviors for coping with problems in the regular classroom.
3. The counselor will meet briefly once every six weeks
   with classroom teachers to help them respond in positive ways to student coping behaviors.

Form J

MANAGEMENT OF IMPLEMENTATION ACTIVITIES

Activity	Person Responsible	Resources or Support Needed	Expected Completion Date
1. LD students selected, scheduled for mainstreaming.	Resource teacher Principal		August 15, 19___
2. Two-day awareness in-service session held.	Resource teacher Principal	Staff development guidelines	September 15, 19___
3. Two-day training session for volunteer teachers held.	Resource teacher Principal	Staff development guidelines	September 25, 19___
4. Resource teacher supplies classroom teachers with student profiles.	Resource teacher	Principal	September 30, 19___
5. LD students begin regular classes.	Principal		October 1, 19___
6. Counseling sessions with LD students begin.	Counselor	Principal	October 15, 19___ (Held for six consecutive weeks)
7. Resource teacher conferences with teachers begin.	Resource teacher	Principal	October 31, 19___ (Held on a monthly basis through May)
8. Counselor conferences with teachers begin.	Counselor	Principal	November 15, 19___ (Held on an every-six-weeks basis through May)
9. Individual student—counselor conferences begun.	Counselor	Principal	December 1, 19___ (Held on a monthly basis through May)
10. Midyear general faculty awareness session held	Resource teacher Principal		January 15, 19___
11. Analysis of student achievement progress conducted.	Resource teacher Classroom teachers	Principal	May 15, 19___

Form K

EVALUATION CRITERIA FOR IMPLEMENTATION PLAN

Criteria	Acceptable	Not Acceptable	Comment
All aspects of the plan are clearly and simply stated.			
Plan has overall acceptance by the faculty.			
Each faculty member involved has had an opportunity for input into the plan.			
The plan is a reasonable expectation of what the faculty can actually do.			
Objectives are consistent with and make concrete the expectations of the statements of general direction.			
Implementation activities for each objective are sufficient for achieving the intent of the objective.			
Activities are realistic in terms of what the staff can and are willing to do.			
Leadership and responsibility for all activities are assigned to person(s) who are qualified and willing to conduct them.			
Time allotted to completion of activities seems reasonable in terms of activity requirements and staff capabilities.			
Implementation activities provide for sufficient coordination of individual effort among staff members, i.e resource teacher, classroom teacher, counselor, and principal.			

_____APPENDICES

APPENDIX A

STUDENT PROFILE
LEARNING PROBLEM IDENTIFICATION SHEET
INSTRUCTIONAL ADJUSTMENT SHEET
EVALUATION OF INSTRUCTIONAL ADJUSTMENT SHEET
INSTRUCTIONAL ADJUSTMENT SUMMARY SHEET

STUDENT PROFILE

Name _____ C.A. _____ Date _____

1. Test Results:

    SIT

    M.A. _____ IQ _____

    WRAT

    Spelling _____ Math _____ Reading _____

    PIAT

    Math _____ Reading Recog. _____ Reading Comp. __

    Spelling _____ General Info. _____ Total __

2. Weaknesses:

3. Strengths:

4. Specific areas of needed remediation:

LEARNING PROBLEM IDENTIFICATION SHEET

Student _____ Teacher _____

1. State what it is that students in the class will be doing. What *activities* will they be engaged in? What materials will they be expected to use? What performance(s) will they be expected to demonstrate?

2. Based on your observations, judgment, and information from the resource teacher, what do you anticipate will be the *learning problems* or obstacles the LD student will face in achieving this knowledge or skill?

INSTRUCTIONAL ADJUSTMENT SHEET

1. Describe *instructional adjustment(s)* devised to compensate for anticipated learning problems, to enhance learning of LD student. Tell what you intend to do, how you intend to do it, and how you expect your adjustments to meet the needs of the LD student.

2. Describe how you will *evaluate* the effectiveness of your instructional adjustments.

EVALUATION OF INSTRUCTIONAL ADJUSTMENT SHEET

1. What evidence do you have that the student did (or did not) benefit from the adjustment(s)? Attach results of tests or questionnaires.

Objective Evidence

Subjective Evidence

2. How do you account for the success or failure of the adjustment(s)? To what extent were you able to implement the adjustment(s) as you planned?

3. What additional adjustment would you consider making to enhance the performance of the LD student?

INSTRUCTIONAL ADJUSTMENT SUMMARY SHEET

Student Name _____

Performance Problems	Instructional Adjustments	Outcome
1.		

APPENDIX B

**SUGGESTED INSTRUCTIONAL
ADJUSTMENTS FOR LD STUDENTS**

SUGGESTED INSTRUCTIONAL
ADJUSTMENTS FOR LD STUDENTS

The following list represents an effort to summarize some ideas for working with LD children in a regular classroom. The list is by no means an exclusive one; teachers are encouraged to generate and try out additional ideas. Any one or a combination of the ideas listed may be used as a basis for adjusting instruction to better meet the needs of LD students.

A. Adjust type, difficulty, and amount of sequence of material required for LD students by:

1. Giving them a lesser amount than the rest of the class; i.e. fewer math problems, fewer pages to read, etc.

2. Breaking their assignments down into short tasks. Many of these children do well if they are provided with short assignments followed by immediate feedback. If LD students concentrate well for three minutes, provide them with a series of three-minute tasks with a break between each. If they can do only one math problem correctly, give them only one, and after they have succeeded at that for several days, increase the number to two, and so on. If they do only the first one or two questions on a page correctly, it may be that their attention is caught by all the material on the page and they would do better with a series of individual questions, each on its own page. A classmate or older student should be able to prepare this for the LD child.

3. Giving them only one (or few) questions at a time during testing.

4. Including in their assignments only that material which is absolutely necessary for them to learn.

5. Checking or underlining for them textbook passages that contain the most important facts — using markers to tell them to start or stop an assignment.

6. Giving them specific questions to guide their reading and, if necessary, showing them the exact paragraphs where information can be found.

7. Establishing only a few modest goals for LD students.

Develop with them the ways you attempt to reach those goals, the things they will have to do.

8. Making certain the students' desks are free from all material except what they are working with.
9. Taking up the students' work as soon as it is completed.
10. Keeping the number of practice items on any skill to a minimum.
11. Changing activities *before* the student's attention is gone; watching for early signs of attention loss.
12. Giving students several alternatives in both obtaining and reporting information — tapes, interviews, reading, experience, or making something, etc.
13. Having frequent, even if short, one-to-one conferences with students; helping them to restate what they are responsible for and assessing their progress toward completion of work.

B. Adjust space for LD children by:
1. Permitting them to do their work in a quiet uncrowded corner of the room or even in the hall outside the room if they choose to do so. However, do not isolate them against their will.
2. Placing them close to the teacher for more immediate help when they need it.
3. Placing them next to students who can help them when needed.
4. Separating them from students who are most likely to distract them.
5. Letting them choose the area of the room where they can concentrate best.

C. Adjust work time for LD students by:
1. Giving them a longer time than other class members to complete assignments.
2. Letting them work at reading and writing assignments for short periods of time, perhaps just ten or fifteen minutes, depending on their ability to concentrate, followed by other types of activities for short periods of time.
3. Setting up a specific schedule for LD students so that they know what to expect.

4. Keeping work periods short; gradually lengthening them as the student begins to cope.

5. Alternating quiet and active time; having short periods of each; making movement as purposeful as possible.

D. Adjust grouping for LD students by:

1. Matching LD students with peer helpers who can help them by:

   a. Making certain they understand directions of assignments.

   b. Reading important directions and essential material to them.

   c. Drilling them orally on what they need to know, i.e. multiplication tables, state capitals, and parts of speech, etc.

   d. Orally summarizing important textbook passages for them.

   e. Writing down answers to tests and assignments for them.

   f. Working with them in a joint assignment.

   g. Criticizing their work for them, making suggestions for improvement.

2. Formulate a small work group of three or four students, including one LD student. Hold all members of the group responsible for making certain that each group member completes assignments successfully.

E. Adjust presentation and evaluation modes for students.

Some of us learn better by seeing, some by listening, some by feeling, and some by a combination of approaches. Some children reinforce their weaker sensory channel by utilizing a multisensory approach, whereas others are overloaded by this system and do better if they learn through their most functional sensory system. Find out how the LD students learn best.

1. If they are primarily auditory learners, adjust mode of presentation for them by:

   a. Giving verbal as well as written directions in assignments.

   b. Taping important reading material for students to listen to as they read a passage. Tape only essential information. Keep it short! Teacher or another student might do the taping.

c. Putting assignment directions on tape so that students can replay them when needed.

d. Giving students oral rather than written tests. Teacher or another student can do this.

e. Having students drill on essential information using tape recorder, reciting information into recorder, and playing it back.

f. Using published audio tapes with students.

g. Having students drill aloud to themselves or to another student.

h. Dictating information to a recorder (another student) or into a tape recorder.

i. Having another student read important information to LD students.

j. Having students read important information aloud to themselves or to another student.

k. Having students reauditorize silently, vocalizing material inside their heads.

l. Having students repeat words aloud (or silently) while writing them down on paper to keep from leaving out words or phrases.

m. Having students close their eyes and try to hear words or information, repeating to themselves in order to block out distractions.

2. If they are primarily visual learners, adjust the mode of presentation for them by:

a. Having students use flash cards printed in bold bright colors.

b. Having students close their eyes and try to *visualize* words or information in their heads, see things in their minds.

c. Providing visual clues on chalkboard for all verbal directions.

d. Having students write down notes and memos to themselves concerning important words, concepts, and ideas.

APPENDIX C

SAMPLE LD STUDENT
LEARNING PROBLEM IDENTIFICATION SHEET

SAMPLE LD STUDENT
INSTRUCTIONAL ADJUSTMENT SHEET

SAMPLE LD STUDENT
EVALUATION OF INSTRUCTIONAL ADJUSTMENT SHEET

Sample

LD STUDENT
LEARNING PROBLEM IDENTIFICATION SHEET

Student _____*Sam*_____ Teacher *Science/Social Studies*

1. State what it is that students in the class will be doing. What *activities* will they be engaged in? What materials will they be expected to use? What performance(s) will they be expected to demonstrate?
   • Students will view film on air pollution.
   • Students will read textbook chapter on air pollution.
   • Students will complete worksheet defining air pollution, listing six ways man pollutes and listing five adverse affects of pollution on man.
2. Based on your observations, judgement, and information from the resource teacher, what do you anticipate will be the *learning problem* or obstacles the LD student will face in achieving this knowledge or skill?
   1. Sam will have difficulty reading the text material.
   2. Sam's short attention span will not allow him to get involved in lengthy activities, particularly writing activities.

Sample

**LD STUDENT
INSTRUCTIONAL ADJUSTMENT SHEET**

1. Describe *instructional adjustment(s)* devised to compensate for anticipated learning problems, to enhance learning of LD student. Tell what you intend to do, how you intend to do it, and how you expect your adjustments to meet the needs of the LD student.
   - Give Sam several (no more than 3) specific questions to guide his viewing of the film. Have him repeat the questions to be certain he understands what he is to look for.
   - Question him orally (and briefly) after the film to check his understanding.
   - Underline for Sam the textbook passages that are most helpful to answering the questions on the worksheet.
   - Have Sam write out the definition to air pollution, one way man pollutes, and one effect of pollution. Have a peer helper record, from Sam's dictation, additional causes and effects.
2. Describe how you will *evaluate* the effectiveness of your instructional adjustments.
   - Quality of Sam's responses to questions about the film.
   - Successful completion of the worksheet.
   - Observation of Sam's persistence and cooperation with peer helper in completing assigned tasks.

Sample

LD STUDENT
EVALUATION OF INSTRUCTIONAL ADJUSTMENT SHEET

1. What evidence do you have that the student did (or did not) benefit from the adjustment(s)? Attach results of tests or questionnaires.

Objective Evidence

- Sam completed the worksheet successfully.

Subjective Evidence

- Sam seemed to enjoy the film and had little trouble summarizing the content.
- Sam had considerable difficulty reading even the limited passages assigned and took longer at the task than anticipated. However, he was persistent and used his peer helper as needed.

2. How do you account for the success or failure of the adjustment(s)? To what extent were you able to implement the adjustment(s) as you planned?
   - Adding structure to Sam's activities and restricting the scope of his tasks seems to have helped him complete his assignment.

3. What additional adjustments would you consider making to enhance the performance of the LD student?
   - Experiment with varying the length of Sam's work periods to determine his most productive times.

Sample

LD STUDENT
LEARNING PROBLEM IDENTIFICATION SHEET

Student _____*Sam*_____ Teacher _____*Science*_____

1. State what it is that students in the class will be doing. What activities will they be engaged in? What materials will they be expected to use? What performance(s) will they be expected to demonstrate?

   Students will be able to name, remove, and replace the six major parts of the digestive system in sequential order, by using an unbreakable model of the human body as a reference.

2. Based on your observations and judgment, and information from the resource teacher, what do you anticipate will be the *learning problem* or obstacles the LD student will face in achieving this knowledge or skill?
   1. He has difficulty following directions accurately.
   2. His manipulative skills are poor.
   3. He has problems in placing things in sequential order.

Sample

LD STUDENT
INSTRUCTIONAL ADJUSTMENT SHEET

1. Describe *instructional adjustment(s)* devised to compensate for anticipated learning problems, to enhance learning of LD student. Tell what you intend to do, how you intend to do it, and how you expect your adjustments to meet the needs of the LD student.

    Sam and other class members will observe the teacher as she names, removes, and replaces the parts of the digestive system in sequential order. To reinforce the parts, a mimeographed sheet of the system will be passed out, and each student will be asked to color the parts — each a different color. Sam will repeat this. The teacher will observe Sam during this time and repeat the parts to him as he colors them. Sam will then label the parts using a chart while the other students locate the parts in their textbook.

    Sam will practice naming, removing, and replacing each of the parts of the digestive system with the teacher or another student in a quiet area of the room while other students complete coloring and locating the parts to be labeled from their textbooks.

    As directions are given to Sam, he will orally repeat them to the teacher before moving to the next activity. During a review by the teacher, the students will repeat aloud after each part is named. Students will then name, remove, and replace the six major parts of the system as they are called on.

2. Describe how you will *evaluate* the effectiveness of your instructional adjustments.

    Adjustments will be considered effective if Sam can name, remove and replace the six major parts of the digestive system.

Sample

LD STUDENT
EVALUATION OF INSTRUCTIONAL ADJUSTMENT SHEET

1. What evidence do you have that the student did (or did not) benefit from the adjustment(s)? Attach results of tests or questionnaries.

Objective Evidence

Sam benefitted from the lesson. He followed the oral directions and knows the parts of the digestive system because he named, removed, and replaced them.

Subjective Evidence

2. How do you account for the success or failure of the adjustment(s)? To what extent were you able to implement the adjustment(s) as you planned?

    Sam was successful because he has a high interest in science and the adjustments planned for him helped him overcome his learning difficulties.

3. What additional adjustments would you consider making to enhance the performance of the LD student?

    1. Practice copying short assignments from the board and turning in short, written homework assignments, increasing the amount gradually.

    2. Read one paragraph at a time, in science text (to a peer helper) paraphrasing the content before reading further.

APPENDIX D

SAMPLE SCIENCE VOCABULARY CONTRACT
SAMPLE LEARNING CONTRACT

Sample

SCIENCE VOCABULARY CONTRACT

Activities I will complete to help me learn the parts of a flower.

Signed _____
(Student's Name)

Activity I
   A. Label a drawing of the flower parts while listening to a tape that will spell out the words and describe shapes, colors, and location of each part of the flower. You can get the tape from the teacher.
   B. Bring your labeled drawing to the teacher after you finish. Do not go on to Activity II before seeing your teacher.
   Due Date/Time _____ Teacher's Initials _____

Activity II
   A. Spell each part of the flower aloud eight times to your peer helper without looking at the word. Check off the block beside each word after you have spelled it correctly eight times. Get the list of words from your teacher.
   B. Bring checked sheet to teacher before going to Activity III.
   Due Date/Time _____ Teacher's Initials _____

Activity III
   A. Without using the tape recorder, label a drawing of the flower.
   B. Bring the labeled drawing to the teacher.
   Due Date/Time _____ Teacher's Initials _____

_____
(Teacher's Signature)

If the above line is signed, you have successfully and satisfactorily completed this contract, and I congratulate you on your good work.

Teacher's Notes

This science vocabulary contract is designed for an LD student who is an auditory learner. This student also has difficulty organizing his thoughts and following directions.

The contract revolves around identification of parts of a flower and around correct spelling of the parts. The number of words should preferably be limited to five (5) but should be no more that eight (8).

Each activity should be explained to the LD student either by the teacher or peer helper, since he has trouble following directions.

Instructions on how to use the tape recorder should be given if he does not know how to operate it. Before the student starts an activity, he or she must check with the teacher. At that time, the teacher can readily see if directions are being followed.

The following should be prepared before contract is given:

1. Drawing and tape for Activity I.
2. Check sheet with block beside word for Activity II.

Give positive comments, praise, and smile or nod of approval concerning this student's work. His self-concept needs to be improved, and after each activity this positiveness can be reinforcing. The peer helper can also provide positive comments.

Finished work done by the LD student should be attached to the contract, so that revisions can be made if necessary.

Sample

LEARNING CONTRACT

(The following is a learning contract format that can be used in any subject area. The format can be used by LD students with problems in reading, writing, and in organizing and sequencing information. The contract provides a variety of ways for the LD student to use his learning strengths in obtaining and reporting information.)

I,_____ , agree to complete the following work to the best of my ability. My teacher,_____, and I will together decide what my grade on this work will be when I am finished. I promise to be finished with this work by_____ .

1. What I am responsible for (teacher decides):

2. How I plan to do the work (teacher and student decide together):

A. *Books, Magazines, News-papers, etc., I Will Use*	*Where Located*	*Exact Pages*	*Exact Paragraph*	*Who Will Help Me*
1.				
2.				
3.				
4.				
5.				

B. *Filmstrips, Records, Tapes I Will Use*	*Where Located*	*Who Will Help Me*	*When I Can Use Them*
1.			
2.			
3.			
4.			

LEARNING CONTRACT *(continued)*

C.	Pictures or Charts I Can Use	Where Located	Who Will Help Me	When I Can Use Them
1.				
2.				
3.				
4.				

D. People I Can Use	Where I Can Find Them	When They Can Help Me
1.		
2.		
3.		
4.		

E. Games I Can Play	Where I Can Find Them	Where I Can Play Them	Who Will Help Me
1.			
2.			
3.			
4.			

F. Things I Can Observe	Where I Can Observe Them	When I Can Observe
1.		
2.		
3.		
4.		

LEARNING CONTRACT*(continued)*

G. *Other Resources I Can Use*	*Where I Can Find Them*	*When I Can Use Them*	*Who Will Help*
1.			
2.			
3.			
4.			

3. Who I will report information to: Teacher, other students.
4. How I will report information (explain to the teacher):
    1. In writing
    2. Pictures, graph, chart
    3. Orally
    4. Make something
    5. Role playing
    6. Tape recorder
    7. Other (list)

Student Signature_____

Teacher Signature_____

APPENDIX E

SAMPLE LEARNING ACTIVITY PACKAGE

SAMPLE LEARNING CENTER — CONCENTRATION

Sample
LEARNING ACTIVITY PACKAGE

The Heart

Note To Teacher: Depending on the nature of the student's disability, the teacher may need to divide this learning activity package (LAP) into several short LAPs, each organized around one objective.

Introduction: During the next few days you will be learning about the heart and how the blood travels through the body. Some of the activities will be short while others will take more time and study.

Directions

1. Go over this LAP with the teacher before you begin working.
2. Portions of this LAP have been tape recorded for your use if you need it. See the teacher.
3. If you need help, ask _____ (student's name) or the teacher.
4. Always talk to the teacher when directions tell you to.

Are you ready to learn about the heart? If so —

Get Ready!
Set!
Go!

Objective 1

You are to learn to identify the following parts of the heart:

1. Veins	5. Ventricle
2. Arteries	6. Valves
3. Vena cava	7. Pulmonary artery
4. Atria	8. Pulmonary veins

Learning these words will be done by choosing *two* of the *three* following activities:

Activities

1. View the filmstrip with tape on the heart. Use the Autovance® machine. (If an Autovance is unavailable, use a filmstrip viewer and tape recorder.) Check each part of heart in the above list as it is described in the filmstrip. Do not worry at this point about what the function of each part is.
2. Using the labeled model of the heart, locate and name parts of the heart with a peer partner. Do this many times until you can do it perfectly at least *twice* in a row.
3. Label the diagram of the heart using the teacher's example located on the bulletin board. Then practice labeling the diagram from memory until you can do it perfectly *twice* in a row.

Go tell the teacher when you think you can identify all the parts.

Objective 2

Now that you can identify the heart you are ready to learn the *function* of each, what each one does.

Do *two* of the three following activities to help you learn more about each part of the heart.

GOOD! YOU KNOW THEM ALL!

_____

Teacher's Signature

CHECKUP
TIME

Activities

1. Replay the filmstrip and tape on the heart. After the function of each part is described, stop the tape and repeat to yourself in your own words the function of that part. Do this *at least three times* for each part. Do not worry about learning them all at one time. Work on two or three until you know them well.

2. _____ (student's name) can work with you on learning the functioning of the parts described in your textbook. Have _____ (student's name) read about the function to you. Then describe the function back to him in your own words. Do this until you can tell about all the parts. Then let _____ (student's name) practice describing the functions to you until he knows them all.

3. Identify each part of the heart from its description. Go to the teacher for the set of flash cards with the parts on one side and the description on the other. Drill yourself until you can name each part from the description.

4. Use the teacher-prepared drill tape. Go to the teacher for the tape. Each part of the heart is described. Play the description, stop the tape and repeat to yourself. Then replay the description to check your answer. Practice! Practice! Practice!

When you have completed your activities and feel you understand the functions of the heart, try to do this checkup. The answers are on the *last* page, but *do not* look until you have finished the checkup.

_____ 1. A blood vessel that carries fresh blood away from the heart.

_____ 2. The two upper chambers of the heart.

_____ 3. The large artery that takes blood from the heart to the lungs.

_____ 4. One of the veins through which the blood flows from

a. Pulmonary artery
b. Ventricle
c. Artery
d. Vein
e. Atria
f. Vena cava
g. Pulmonary vein
h. Valves

the lungs back to the heart.
_____ 5. A blood vessel that carries blood from all parts of the body back to the heart and lungs.
_____ 6. Either of the two lower chambers of the heart.

Check your answers on page 140.
How do you feel about your checkup results? Check one.

Share your results with the teacher. He will be interested in your results.

Objective 3

Now that you know how the different parts of the heart function, you are ready to learn how the blood circulates through the heart.

Activities (Do 1. Choose either 2 or 3.)

1. Listen to the tape describing the path blood takes through the heart and body. Using the diagram that the teacher has prepared, trace the path with your finger as you listen.
2. Trace a drop of blood through the heart by placing arrows on the following diagram. Check your work with the diagram on the last page of this LAP. If you made any mistakes, correct them, get a new diagram from the teacher, and try again. Practice this as much as you need to.

3. Using a blank tape, record the path a drop of blood takes through the heart. Name each part of the heart as the blood enters it. Do this from memory and have your teacher check it. Practice with your tape as much as you need to. Have the teacher sign his name if he feels you have successfully met your objective.

_____

(Teacher's Signature)

Objective 4

You will learn how the pulse rate is different following normal and strenuous activities.

This part of the package can be a lot of fun. Enjoy discovering how each individual can speed up his own pulse rate through physical activities.

Activities (Choose one of the following.)

Record Your Findings

1. Choose a peer partner and take his pulse:

a. While he is sitting calm. ___Times a minute
b. After "running in place" for one
   minute. ___Times a minute
2. Choose a peer partner and by using a stethoscope, count the
   number of times his heart beats per minute:
   a. Following a walk around the
      room. ___Times a minute
   b. Following a series of twenty
      jumping jacks. ___Times a minute

Record your results on the above activity you chose.

Self-Check

(Circle the correct response.)

1. Pulse rate will be (slower, faster) than normal after running around the block.
2. The pulse rate will be (slower, faster) than normal after
   doing exercises.

Check to see if your responses are correct. Answers are on the
last page.

You have completed your package! Do you think you understand the heart any better now? _____

Have your teacher sign below showing you have completed
all the activities.

_____
(Teacher's Signature)

ANSWER PAGE

Objective 1

    1. c — Artery
    2. e — Atria
    3. a — Pulmonary artery
    4. g — Pulmonary vein
    5. d — Vein
    6. b — Ventricle

Objective 3

Objective 4

    1. Faster
    2. Faster

Sample
LEARNING CENTER – CONCENTRATION

I. Specific Purpose:

The purpose of this learning center is to help the LD student learn specific terms and their meanings in any subject area.

II. Construction:

In order to make this center, the following materials are needed:

1. Twelve small envelopes (manila)
2. Two large envelopes (manila)
3. Large poster board (colored, if possible)
4. Markers for numbers
5. Twelve blank cards or twelve pieces of paper

The large poster board should be folded so that two sides extend to the front; the center should then stand alone. Paste, glue, or tape one large envelope on each extended side as shown on the diagram. (The self-test is in the right envelope and various groups of words and meanings are in the left envelope.) The twelve small envelopes should be placed in the center area and arranged in chronological order, as shown in the diagram with a number on each. The title can be written or printed above the small envelopes.

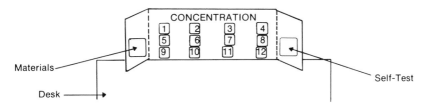

Six words and their meanings can be placed on cards in the middle area of the center, one word for each of six envelopes, one word meaning for each of six remaining envelopes. The words and meanings should be mixed up over the board. A different color can be taped, glued, or pasted on the back of each card; the colors on the back of the words should correspond with the colors on the back of the meanings.

III. What the LD Student Does at the Center:

The student selects a word or meaning from an envelope. He or she then looks for a corresponding meaning. If the colors on the back of the cards are the same, the student knows he or she has a correct match, and he or she is immediately reinforced. If not, the student replaces the selection and starts over until one corresponds. The corresponding words and meanings should be placed on the table in front of the student, not back into the envelopes. A process of trial and error continues until the student has removed all of the cards from the board. This process can be repeated until the student is ready to take the self-test located on the right side of the board. It should be a matching type, since the center itself concerns word association and their meanings. The student can go over the board again before taking the self-test if he feels he needs to, or until he masters 90 percent of the words. The student can take a teacher-prepared test when he feels he is ready for it. Review of words and their meanings and new words can be introduced in the center.

IV. How the Center Meets the Needs of the LD Student:

This center can facilitate the primary mode of visual learning, self-pacing, and self-evaluation and provide for immediate reinforcement.

V. Evaluation:

A matching or multiple choice type test should be given the LD student after he has gone over the board and feels he is ready to be graded.

BIBLIOGRAPHY

Adolescents and Learning Disabilities. Film distributed by Lawren Publications, P.O. Box 1542, Burlingame, California 94010; rental cost $30, purchase price $330.

Anderson, Robert P.: *The Child with Learning Disabilities and Guidance.* Guidance Monograph Series. Boston, Houghton Mifflin Co., 1970.

Blackburn, Jack E. and Powell, W. Conrad: *One at a Time All at Once.* Pacific Palisades, California, Goodyear Publishing Co., 1976.

Canfield, Jack and Wells, Harold C.: *One Hundred Ways to Enhance Self-Concept in the Classroom.* Englewood Cliffs, New Jersey, Prentice-Hall, 1976.

Chase, Larry: *The Other Side of the Report Card: A How-to-Do-It Program for Affective Education.* Pacific Palisades, California, Goodyear Publishing Co., 1975.

Chesler, Mark and Fox, Robert: *Role-Playing Methods in the Classroom.* Chicago, Science Research Associates, 1966.

Deshler, Donald: Psycho-social characteristics of learning disabled adolescents. *Learning Disabilities in the Secondary School.* Title III. Curriculum Development for Secondary Learning Disabilities. A conference report sponsored by Montgomery County, Pennsylvania, Intermediate Unit 23, March, 1975.

Drew, Christopher J.: *Kids Accepted Here: Activities for the Classroom.* Merrimac, Massachusetts, Network of Innovative Schools, 1975.

Dunn, Rita and Dunn, Keith: *Practical Approaches to Individualized Instruction.* West Nyack, New York, 1972.

Dunn, Lloyd, M. and Markwardt, Frederick C.: *Peabody Individual Achievement Test.* Circle Pines, Minnesota, American Guidance Service, 1970.

Durost, Walter, N., Bixler, Harold H., Wrightstone, J. Wayne, Prescott, George A., and Balow, Irving H.: *Metropolitan Achievement Test.* New York, Harcourt Brace Jovanovich, 1975.

Hagin, Rosa A.: How do we find him? In Schloss, Ellen (Ed.): *The Educator's Enigma: The Adolescent with Learning Disabilities.* San Rafael, California, Academic Therapy Publications, 1971.

Hammill, Donald and Wiederholt, J. Lee: *The Resource Room: Rationale and Implementation.* Philadelphia, Buttonwood Farms, 1972.

Hawisher, Margaret F.: *The Resource Room: An Access to Excellence.* Lancaster, South Carolina, Region V Educational Services Center, 1975.

143

Hawisher, Margaret F. and Calhoun, Mary Lynne: *The Resource Room: An Educational Asset for Children with Special Needs.* Columbus, Charles E. Merrill Publishing Co., 1978.

Hayes, Marnell L.: *Oh, Dear, Somebody Said "Learning Disabilities"! A Book for Teachers and Parents.* San Rafael, California, Academic Therapy Publications, 1975.

Humes, Charles W.: The secondary school counselor and learning disabilities. *School Counselor,* 1974.

Jastak, J.F. and Jastak, S.R.: *Wide Range Achievement Test.* Wilmington, Delaware, Guidance Associates of Delaware, 1965.

Kapfer, Philip G. and Ovard, Glen F.: *Preparing and Using Individualized Learning Packages for Upgraded Continuous Progress Education.* Englewood Cliffs, New Jersey, Educational Technology Publications, 1971.

Kiester, Edwin. A Parent's Guide to Learning Disabilities. *Today's Health,* 53: 22-5, 1975.

Madden, Richard, Gardner, Eric F., Rudman, Herbert C., Karlsen, Bjorn, and Merwin, Jack C.: *Stanford Achievement Test.* New York, Harcourt Brace Jovanovich, 1975.

Office of Programs for the Handicapped: *Procedures for Survey, Screening, Evaluation, Placement, and Dismissal of Children Into/Out of Programs for the Handicapped.* Columbia, South Carolina, South Carolina State Department of Education, 1976.

Office of Programs for the Handicapped: *The Resource Room.* Columbia, South Carolina, South Carolina Department of Education, 1974.

Piers, Ellen B. and Harris, Dale B.: *Piers-Harris Self-Concept Scale.* Nashville, Tennessee, Counselor Recordings and Tests, 1969.

Schloss, Ellen (Ed.): *The Educator's Enigma: The Adolescent with Learning Problems.* San Rafael, California, Academic Therapy Publications, 1971.

Simon, Sidney B., Howe, Leland W., and Kirschenbaum, Howard: *Values Clarification: A Handbook of Practical Strategies for Teachers and Student.* New York, Hart Publishing Co., 1972.

Slosson, Richard L. *Slosson Intelligence Test.* New York, Slosson Educational Publications, 1963.

Stenner, A. Jackson and Katzenmeyer, William G.: *Self-Observation Scale.* Durham, North Carolina, National Testing Service, 1975.

Tiegs, Ernest W. and Clark, Willis W.: *California Achievement Test.* Monterey, California, McGraw-Hill Book Co., 1970.

A Walk in Another Pair of Shoes. Filmstrip-tape distributed by CANHC, P.O. Box 604, Main Office, Los Angeles, California 90055; cost $7.90.

Wiederholt, J. Lee: *A Report on Secondary School Programs for the Learning Disabled.* Leadership Training Institute in Learning Disabilities, Department of Special Education, University of Arizona, Phoenix, 1975.

Wilcox, Evangeline: In Anderson, Luriel E. (Ed.): *Helping the Adolescent with the Hidden Handicap.* Belmont, California, Fearon Pub-

lishers/Lear Siegler, 1970.
Voight, Ralph Claude: *Invitation to Learning: The Learning Center Handbook.* Washington, D.C., Acropolis Books, 1971.

INDEX

147